MAMA SAID

Rosie Lee Walker's Journey

September 3, 1920 — April 13, 2015
(Age 94)

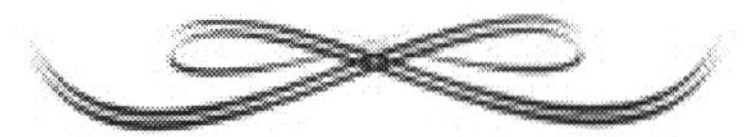

The Way It Was 1920 -2015
Moving From Louisiana to
Los Angeles, Ca.

Arranged and Edited by
Rosie Lee Walker's Family Members

Mama Said

ISBN: 978-1540733764

First Edition
Manufactured in the United States of America
Cover Design by Creative By Design, Kim Lewis, Corona, Ca.
Interior Design by Miriam Pace

Library of Congress Control Number 2016911936

To Mitsy:

I hope you enjoy my 2nd published Book About my mom's Life.

God Bless,
Ethel Mae Lewis

About the Author

Mrs. Ethel Mae Lewis was born in Louisiana in the early 1940's. After her father was discharged from World War II the family moved to Los Angeles. Mrs. Lewis arrived just in time to start her first year of kindergarten.

Mrs. Lewis is also the author of Ethel Mae's Cookbook. It has so many of her mother and other southern family members' recipes in it.

She was married once and to this union was four sons.

Mrs. Lewis, who has survived both breast cancer and lymphoma, hopes her reading audience enjoys her book on the life of her parents and family.

Dedication

I would like to dedicate this novel, "MAMA SAID" to my grandparents, parents, children, grandchildren, and future generations. To the baby boomers of the past, I was part of an era as a youth where we had few Black heroes to emulate. Thank God, today we have many Black heroes.

Now, I have been blessed with the opportunity of writing a novel on my Mother Rosie Lee Walker and her life to pass on to her family.

Rosie Lee Edwards-Walker in life was a sweet, honest, and giving person who left a rich legacy to her family that will live on forever.

My sisters and I was fortunate as children to have the experience of being raised by a very strong and unique African-American mother. Her wisdom and foresight helped mold us into the women we are today. My parents taught us discipline, respect, love, compassion, and pride.

Ethel Mae Walker-Lewis
Daughter of Hanspard and Rosie Lee Walker
Granddaughter of Charles and Virginia Edwards

Acknowledgement

I would like to acknowledge Mrs. Rosie Lee Edwards-Walker for her strength and teaching her children if it is for right to always stand their grounds and not back down. Rosie Lee Walker lived ninety-four blessed years and one of her greatest loves was her daughters, grandchildren, family and the church. It was an honor to have written a novel on the life of our mother.

We are thankful she accomplished her dreams and goals she set out for. Both of our parents were caring, loving, brainy, and brilliant people. We also thank her for instilling in all of her children to be strong, faithful, and loving. Our parents gave us a foundation which made all of their children believe and hope.

Table of Contents

About the Author 3
Dedication 4
Acknowledgement 5
Table Of Contents 6
Introduction 9
Charles and Virginia Banks-Edwards 12
Charles and Virginia Edwards 13
Quotes of Others Loved 16
Our Ancestry 18
Life on the plantation from 19
Religious and Education Life 23
Transportation 24
Hobbies 25
About Grandma Virginia Edwards 27
How Did Grandma Virginia Edwards 28
How Did Daddy and Mama Meet? 30
Our Father Hanspard Walker's Parents 33
Rosie Lee Walker Was Born With A Veil Over Her Eyes 34
Buttermilk and Cornbread 35
Cleanliness Is Next To Godliness 36
Mama's Hip Dance–1925 38
Mama Goes to Jail–1933 40
Rosie Lee Walker's First Husband 42
Mama Could Dance The Jitterbug 44
Daddy Shipped Off Overseas To World War II—1942 46

Table of Contents (con't)

Mt. Sariah Baptist Church. 47
The Family Move From Louisiana To L.A.—1947.. 48
Massive Tornado Hits Cotton Valley, Louisiana–1947 56
Mr. and Mrs. I Spy 58
Growing Up In Los Angeles In The 1940s–1950s . 59
Leaving Your Food or Drink 60
Daddy's BBQ & Domino Playing.......................... 62
Central Avenue in Los Angeles 63
The Lincoln Theatre–1950s 64
Burning Hair and Underwear................................ 66
Coca-Cola Building 70
Racism Experienced For the First Time In L.A. –1952 72
Virginia Marie Walker Jones 1952–1982 74
The Catholic Church–1956 75
Huggy Boy and Dolphin's of Hollywood–1956...... 77
The Bill Robinson Theatre, Los Angeles–1957 78
Johnny Otis TV Show 1957–1963 79
The Surprise Baby–1959 80
Atty Murphy, Lil' Mama, Age 12 82
The Freeway Crawler—1962 86
Mama Dancing to Joe Tex 'Ain't Gonna Bump No More'—1977 90
Ethel Mae Won On Two Different TV Game Shows Two Years In A Row—1980s................................ 92
Don't Walk Up On Mama from the Back—1985 94

Table of Contents (con't)

Ethel Mae's Car Accident—1989 96
Tenors, Cook, Dixon, & Young, with Rosie Walker—2003 105
The Dog And Cow Story—2004 107
Daddy's Funeral—2004 109
What Is A Sheet Shaker—2006 113
Surprise Visitors At My House But I Am Not Home—2008 115
Another Blessing By The Williams Brother—2007 117
Kissing Cousins and Betsy Bugs 118
Making Fun Of Anything While Pregnant Is Not A Good Thing 119
Grandma Held Off A Robber—2009 120
The Last Days Of Rosie Lee Walker—2015 122
Rosie Lee Edwards-Walker Funeral April 25, 2015 125
Pearls of Wisdom 128

Introduction

Mama Said is a brilliant dialogue of the way it was in the life of Mrs. Rosie Lee Walker from 1920–2015.

Mama was pretty, had the prettiest smile, elegant dresser, spiritual, sweet and giving, and would give you her last nickel. As a little girl, not more than nine years old, she had learned survival skills better than an adult.

Mama said when she was a little girl an old lady told her she would always have money and never have to work. Until her last days on this earth she always had money and never had to go on any job.

People always liked being around Mom—the young and the old from the time she was a little girl. With her personality and the way she says things, she could have been a comedian and was just as funny as any famous comedian you know, except Mom does not curse. Mom did not say or do things to be funny—it was the way she said it and her facial expression she made that made a person fall out of their chair onto the floor laughing out of control.

Mom was one of the best cooks. Growing up people from all over the neighborhood came over to our house to eat her food. She cooked like she was feeding an army, at all times.

One day our Pastor came over and ate Mom's

food and when he finished he said, "Sister Walker this food taste so good you must have spit in it." Back in the woods in Louisiana 'spit in it' means it taste better than most.

Not only would Rosie Lee Walker want all African Americans to find their place in life but all races with hard work and education. She was a very wise Mom. She always thought wisdom was the key word to make ignorance disappear.

Most of the stories in this book Mama told me, but some I witnessed.

Rosie Lee Walker expired April 13, 2015 at the age of ninety-four years old. She will live in our memory forever. I hope all of my Mom's family, friends and reading audience enjoy reading my book on the life of a great lady.

Charles and Virginia Banks-Edwards

Parents of Rosie Lee Edwards-Walker

The portrait of Grandpa Charles and Grandma Virginia Edwards was painted after their wedding day in 1901.

Charles and Virginia Edwards Eleven Children

1. Pastor Jethro Edwards (Buddy) 1901-1991
2. Willie Mae Edwards Lewis (Cissy) 1904-1998
3. Cora Edwards Washington (Bit) 1905-1997
4. Mary Magdalene Edwards Jackson (Sang) 1909-2013
5. Dave Edwards
6. Martha Edwards
7. Charlie Edwards, Jr.
8. Tommie Edwards
9. Rosie Lee Edwards Walker 1920-2015
10. Sammie Edwards (Duge) 1922-1970
11. A girl was born but never given a name. She expired at 7 weeks old.

Rosie Lee Walker and her five daughters—Ethel Mae Lewis, Juanita Kelly, Atty Murphy, Virginia Jones, and Willa Dasher.

Quotes of Others Loved By Mrs. Rosie Lee Walker

1. Worry Looks Around, Sorry Looks Back, Faith Looks Forward
2. Common Sense Is Seeing Things As They Are And Doing Things As They Ought To Be
3. If **GOD** Is For Us Who Can Be Against Us
4. Sometimes We Hit Rock Bottom But **GOD** Is The Rock At The Bottom
5. Darkness cannot drive out darkness light can do that. Hate cannot drive out hate, only love can do that. *(Dr. Martin Luther King, Jr. 1929-1968)*
6. Education is the most powerful weapon you can use to change the world. *(Nelson Mandela 1918-2013)*
7. No one is born hating another person because of the color of his skin, or his background, or his religion. People must learn to hate, and if they can learn to hate they can be taught to love, for love comes more naturally to the human heart then its opposite. *(Nelson Mandela 1918-2013)*
8. The world will not be destroyed by those who do evil, but by those who watch them without doing anything. *(Albert Einstein 1879-1955)*
9. The size of the obstacle is unimportant, having the courage and conviction to overcome it is im-

portant. *(The Little Rock Nine 1957)*

10. Imagination: The ability to foresee, visualize, and create your idea in your mind is the most powerful resource you have. *(George Washington Carver 1864-1943)*
11. Those who make peaceful revolution impossible will make violent revolution inevitable." *(President John F. Kennedy 1917-1963)*
12. Prejudice is like a hair across your cheek. You can't see it, you can't find it with your fingers, but you keep brushing at it because the feel of it is irritating. *(Marian Anderson 1897-1993)*
13. If you forget your history you will repeat your history.
14. Endless Effort: In order to reach your gold you must continue to strive in spite of interference or treatment. *(Harriet Tubman 1820-1943)*
15. Achievement: those who refuse to place limitations upon themselves will always succeed. *(Thurgood Marshall 1908-1993)*
16. Never give up: You can do anything but do your best. When a job is once begun be it large or small, do it right or not at all. Always kill the word can't and whip the words could not.

Our Ancestry

In 1901 our grandfather, Charles Edwards married Virginia Banks Edwards. They lived in Cotton Valley, Louisiana until their last days. The city of Cotton Valley is located in the Webster Parish area. Louisiana is the only state in America that has parishes, fifty-two to be exact. Cotton Valley was established in the mid-19th century, but was not incorporated until 1944.

Grandpa Charles and Grandma Virginia's parents were ex-slaves. Our grandparents and their children were sharecroppers on Old Man Hayes' Plantation.

Sharecropping along with tenant farming was a dominant form in the South from the 1870's to the 1950's, among blacks and whites. Sharecroppers worked a section of the plantation, independently, usually growing cotton, tobacco, rice, sugar and other cash crops and received half of the parcel's output.

After our ancestors landed in America they were sold to white slave masters and often time sold a lot of times to different slave masters.

Virginia Banks Edwards was of mixed ancestry with African, Cherokee Indian, and White blood.

In the woods where our grandparents and parents were born, it was not uncommon to have no grass or weeds in front of your house. There was nothing but hard dirt which became as hard as clay dirt. Mama said sometimes they would sweep the dirt with a broom as if it was a wood floor. She said it kept the snakes away.

Life on the plantation from 1865—1940s

Charles and Virginia Banks-Edwards were born in the Webster Parish area of Louisiana during the Reconstruction of the Jim Crow era that began shortly after President Abraham Lincoln signed the Emancipation Proclamation, which ended slavery in 1864. Since very few blacks owned property during slavery, they either served as sharecroppers on white plantations or farms, or they migrated up north. Although slavery had ended, blacks had very few rights, were subject to false imprisonment, could not go to school, vote or own property.

Black males were not allowed to speak out and were subject to many false accusations and lynching throughout the South, including the Webster Parish area of Louisiana during the early 1900's. Sometimes nightriders would lynch a black man and hang him on a tree so that passersby could see. They wanted them to be reminded to "Stay in Your Place."

Almost all black families living in the Jim Crow

era had a male relative who was either shot or killed for speaking out about how blacks were treated or for being falsely accused of some crime. These were the drive by shootings of the 1930's and 1940's.

The Edwards descendants were farmers. Many families planted up to thirty to forty acres of crops. In a good year a farm would produce six bales of cotton.

They also raised corn, which was used as a fresh summer vegetable. It was also used for canning or storing during winter months. Dried corn was used to make meal, grits, and hominy. Corn was also used to feed cattle, and hogs. Persimmons, plums, blackberries and blueberries, mulberries and hickory nuts were also used as fresh food items or made into jellies and preserves or stored for later use.

Part of the pastureland was used to raise livestock, including cattle, horses, mules, hogs, and poultry. Poultry included not only chickens for eggs and fresh meat, but ducks, geese, turkeys, guinea fowls, and bantam chickens. Hogs were used to provide fresh meat, stewed to make lard and crackling, and cured to provide dry salt pork, bacon, jowls, and ham.

Pastureland contained pine, oak, elm, and other hardwood trees that provided firewood for cooking and heating. The area around Shreveport provided much of the South's lumber for building material and paper products. Steel saws and axes were used to chop down trees. Since there were many girls in the family, they did heavy labor just like the boys. Many of the girls would plow. They also served as cotton chopper and pickers, fence makers and menders. Grasses and hay were grown to feed cattle and horses during the winter. Stock ponds were used to provide water for livestock and stocked with fish.

The family would buy granulated sugar, flour, sure jell, and mason jars from the store. Traveling salesmen would come by homes periodically to sell vanilla, lemon, and other extracts as well as spices such as black pepper, nutmeg, and cinnamon.

Before refrigeration, an icebox was used as temporary storage for milk, butter, meat, and other perishable items. Blocks of ice and dry ice were used to keep items that were stored in the ice box cold.

The Edwards women were not only homemakers who took care of their children and grandchildren and relatives, but they were the best cooks.

In the late 1880's through the early 1940's Grandma Virginia and her daughters would awaken before sunrise and prepare breakfast in the kitchen. Cooking was done on a wood burning stove. Cattle were raised to provide meat and milk. Butter was used to season biscuits, grits, flapjacks, cakes teacakes, pies and cobblers.

Usually lard or bacon grease was used to fry chicken, fish, or other meats or to season vegetables and make cornbread. As most women of the house, Grandma Virginia also canned fruits and vegetables that were gathered from the farm. These canned products often supplied the family with all of the vegetables and fruits need for food during the winter.

During the winter months, the smoke house would not only be used to store salted and smoked meats, but fresh meat as well. Hot ashes in the front of the fireplace were used to roast sweet potatoes or peanuts.

Grandma Virginia also sewed most of the family's clothes. Among other things, she quilted, washed and ironed. A wash pot was used to boil white clothes and linen before rinsing.

Grandpa Charles was scared to death of white people. Grandpa and Mama were walking down a road and coming toward them was Old Man Hayes the plantation owner and his wife. In passing Grandpa accidentally touched the wife's shoulder, and almost peed in his pants. The only way Grandpa settled down Old Man Hayes had to let him know it was just an accident and no big deal. In the slavery day era if a black man touched a white female that was like a death wish.

Mama said she thinks the reason Grandpa was like that is because when he was about five years old, in 1879, some Klansmen on horses rolled up in front of his parents' house in the woods, drag one of the older family members out of the house—held grandpa and made him watch while they hung the person on a tree and tar-feather him until he was dead.

What is the definition of Tar and Feather? Tarring and feathering is a form of public humiliation used to enforce unofficial justice or revenge. It is a mob vengeance act.

Liquid tar was either poured or painted onto the person while he was immobilized. Then the victim either had feathers thrown on him or was rolled around on a pile of feathers so that they stuck to the tar.

Mama said she got her ways from Grandma Virginia, born 1883. I am so glad Mama got her ways from grandma. I would not want my mama to almost pee in her pants for accidentally touching or bumping into a white person or any other race. To me a simple apology should be sufficient.

Religious and Education Life

The Edwards family members were Baptist and very active in the church. The church they attended was Mt. Sariah Baptist Church in Cotton Valley, Louisiana. Up until 1955, most churches served as the public school for children through the eighth grade. Those who wanted to attend high school, could not go next door to the white school, they would have to stay with a relative in Shreveport, to attend Booker T. Washington High School which was an all-black school. From Cotton Valley to Shreveport was about fifty miles.

None of Charles and Virginia Banks-Edwards children attended high school because they had to help their parents work Old Man Hayes Plantation. Those who got their education were after they became grown, left home or join the military for World War II. Our father, Hanspard Walker, completed his education after he was discharged from World War II.

Transportation

Before Shreveport was found in 1839, goods and passengers were transported by steamboat. Wagons also had many uses, including the hauling of wood, hay, corn and other produce, as ell as serving as a form of transportation for the family members riding to and from places such as the church or the town.

Since work on the farm had to be done during the day when it was hot, many visits to family members or neighbors were done at night, on a trail and in groups. It was not wise for blacks to walk on highways at night because of harassment by the

Klan, the lynch mob, or nightriders. It was much better to use forest trails, even though they were full of water moccasins, rattle snakes, red wolves, wild boars, and other wild animals.

During World War II, many black men joined the Army and other military services to defeat the Germans and Japanese in both Atlantic and Pacific campaigns. After the war many jobs opened up to blacks.

Hobbies

Charles Edwards and other male children liked to hunt ducks, rabbits, squirrels, coons, possums, armadillos and other wild game. The males also fished for perch and catfish from ponds. After crops were harvested in the fall, a popular pastime in Cotton Valley, Louisiana was the famous Louisiana Hayride where groups of family members and friends would ride in a wagon filled with hay and eat corn and peanuts and drink lemonade.

The females, in addition to raising their children, also canned, sewed, quilted and fished. They always had meals and all types of sweets ready in case company came by.

Our Mom Rosie said Old Man Hayes, the plantation owner and his little daughter who was her age always played together since they were little babies on grandpa's front porch or the yard when Old Man Hayes came by to collect.

When Old Man Hayes daughter Sally became nine years old Mama said things changed. On this particular day Mama said Old Man Hayes walked up to her while she was playing with his daughter and said, "Rosie Lee, you gonna have to put a handle on it."

Mama asked him, "What is a handle?"

He said, "You and Sally are getting to be big girls now you are going to have to start calling her Miss Sally."

Mama said she told him, "I ain't, she is nine years old just like me."

Old Man Hayes goes into the house to report to Grandpa about his daughter. "Charles, Rosie Lee want call Sally Miss Sally."

Mama said, "I did not care if Papa whipped me I was not going to call that girl Miss Sally and we were the same age." Mama said, "I left Louisiana when I was twenty-two years old for California and I was calling her the same name I called her when we were little girls, just plain old Sally."

Mama does not know how lucky she was to be born a girl because the way she was born for just right and not white or any other skin color— had she been born a boy I doubt if a he would have lived one day past eleven years old. Any 'he who was born in the Deep South in the 1920's like Mama would have been lynched, and/or tarred and feathered and they would still be looking for his body in the Mississippi river. My goodness was she lucky to have been born a girl.

About Grandma Virginia Edwards

When I was a little girl Mama told me her mother Virginia Banks-Edwards was born with a different last name and her birth last name was Knuckles, the last name of the slave owner. I asked Mama, "Who changed Grandma Virginia's last name to her present last name?" Mama said, "Baby I don't know I was too little."

In 2004 I moved Mom in with me and in her garage at her house I found an old picture album and in the front of the album was a dark-skin lady. At top of the album it had 'Cousin Honey 100 Year Birthday Celebration. I asked Mama, "Who is Cousin Honey?"

She said, "She is my Mama's first cousin."

How Did Grandma Virginia Edwards Die? 1883-1933

I remember as a little girl asking Mom, "How did Grandma Virginia die?"

She replied, "Baby, Mama can't to talk about it."

When I asked, she had this sad look on her face. Even though I was a little girl I knew if such a question was going to make Mama look that said I could care less if I ever knew how Grandma died and never asked again.

After I moved Mom in with me, one night very late while I was asleep in bed her voice woke me up from her bedroom. To me it sounded as if she was having a nightmare. When I got to her bedroom door she was having a nightmare and I woke her up. When I woke her up and asked her what was the matter, she replied "I was dreaming about rubbing Mama's feet, referring to Grandma Virginia who expired in 1933 when my mother was thirteen years old. I asked, "Why were you rubbing Grandma's feet?"

Mama said when she was thirteen years old there was some big church affair going on. Uncle Boagie was driving Grandpa Charles old 1928 car picking up the first batch of folks and dropping them off at the church, returning and picking up the next group of people to drop them off.

On the second pickup–return to the church in the car was, Uncle Boagie who was the driver, Grandma Virginia, Aunt Mary (Sang), and Uncle Sammie (Duge). The old car hit a big rock and flipped over throwing everybody clear except Grandma Virginia. The car landed on top of her stomach. They took Grandma home and tried to doctor on her, but she got very sick. They packed her up and took her to a hospital in the big city of Shreveport, Louisiana called The Charity Hospital. The Charity Hospital is about fifty miles from where they lived.

Mama said she was visiting Grandma Virginia in the hospital and was at the foot of her bed rubbing her feet. Mama said she thought rubbing her feet made her feel so good it put her to sleep. In the room with Mom was her older brother, Jethro (Buddy), and her older sister Mary (Sang). The nurse walks into the room to let all of them know she had just passed. Mama said all she could remember is running out of the room and running up and down the hall way screaming out of control, and at some point returned to Grandma Virginia's bedside. She said Buddy and Sang came over to her and said, "Rosie Lee, baby we have got to go." The year 2004 was the first time the senior citizen Ethel Mae was told how Grandma Virginia died.

How Did Daddy and Mama Meet?

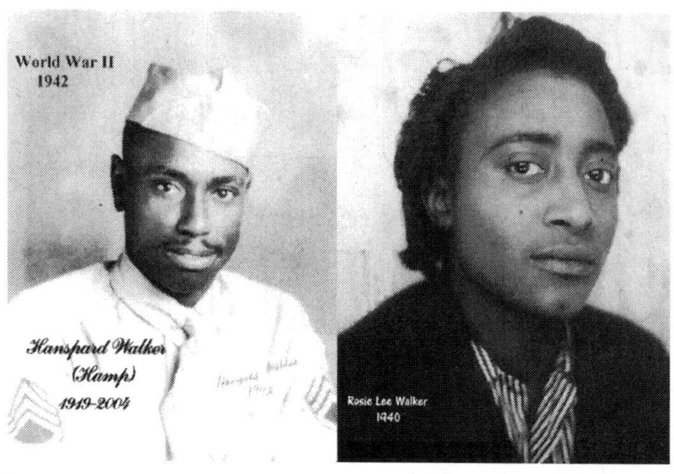

Daddy and Mama married in 1941, before he was shipped off overseas to World War II. Daddy was twenty-two years old and Mama was twenty-one years old. My World War II, father Hanspard Walker and our Mama Rosie Lee Walker are exactly one year apart. They have known each other since they were in diapers.

Daddy was named after his Grandpa Hanspard Duncan, on his mother's side of the family. Nobody calls Daddy by his first name 'Hanspard, everybody calls him by his nickname 'Hamp.

Both their parents were Sharecroppers on Old Man Hayes Plantation. Daddy lived across the road from Mama. All of the little children living in the woods played together growing up. At first they were little children playing together but things changed when Daddy became thirteen years old and Mama twelve years old. Daddy said, "Your Mama was fine and I did not want that children friend stuff no more."

Mama said he tried to kiss her and feel her behind. She said she balled up her fist and hit him as hard as she could on the jaw. She said, "I cold cocked that fool. He fell down on the ground out for the count." Mama said it scared her because he would not move.

The kids ran down the road to get Grandma Mary, his Mom. Mama said Grandma Mary comes running down the road with her white apron on, when she bend over Daddy trying to bring him back she said, "Oh Lord Rosie Lee done killed my boy." After Grandma Mary started patting his face and putting water on it, he came back.

Daddy sure was smitten with Mama, you'd think if some little twelve year old girl can knock out a big thirteen year old boy he would have thought twice before he married her and venture out for another wife. And she knocked him out with just her bare hands not even a weapon.

Daddy said she had so much strength in her right fist she could move a building from its foundation. Daddy once said the only way you are going to get Rosie Lee you have got to get her from the back.

After they married—what if some of Daddy's World War II buddies came over to their house to visit and Daddy did something real stupid and made her deck him and had him down on the floor. You'd think he would have been embarrassed explaining to his buddies how some little exactly 5' woman could put his 6'1' self down on the floor.

Daddy said someone tried to attack Mama and when she got through, the person asked him to help them because Mama was getting the best of the person. Daddy said he told the person, "I am not saying nothing to Rosie Lee, she can do whatever she wants and every man for them self." Daddy said our Mama Rosie had the strength of ten men and the speed of Jessie Owens, and could make the same moves as well as Bruce Lee if anyone tried to mess with her.

Most women prayed no one tried to attack or rob them, but not our mother. Mom was just the opposite, and prayed and hoped anyone tried to attack or rob her as if it was a blessing if they tried. If anyone tried to attack or rob our mother these would have been the exact words out of her mouth, "Oh *Jesus* you knew what woman to send this fool to, oh you is a good *God*"

Our Father Hanspard Walker's Parents

Henry Walker, Jr. (July 31, 1887-July 29, 1940)
Mary Lucinda Duncan-Walker (June 5, 1885--?)

Our Grandpa Henry Walker, Jr. is our Grandma Mary Lucinda Duncan Walker's second husband. Grandpa Henry Walker Jr. was born 1887-1940 and Grandma Mary Lucinda Duncan-Walker was born 1885. I could not find out the year Grandma Mary expired but I was not much older than eleven years old when she expired. Everybody called Grandma Mary by her nickname 'Miss Sister.

Grandpa Henry and Grandma Mary had three children and their names are, Arlanders Walker (Al) 1915-2002, Hanspard Walker (Hamp) 1919-2004, and Ethel Lee Walker-Lewis (Mut) 1922-2000.

I was named after my father's sister, who I call by her nickname 'Aunt Mut.' Her name is Ethel Lee Walker and my name is Ethel Mae Walker, we have different middle names. Both of us married men with the same last name of Lewis, but no relation. Our mother Rosie knew very little about Grandma Mary's first husband, who is not my grandfather.

She said his last name was Mr. Tucker born in the late 1880's and he had two sons, which she knew. Their names are Jessie Tucker (1909-1933), and Reese Tucker (1905-1961).

Rosie Lee Walker Was Born With A Veil Over Her Eyes

Born With A Veil, What Does It Mean?

People who are born with a Veil over their head often have psychic and other supernatural abilities such as seeing ghosts and foretelling the future. Many can predict weather patterns and crop yields.

Being born with a veil is often a subject of mystery and intrigue. So what exactly does it mean? A veiled birth occurs when a child is born and has a portion of the birth membrane remaining around its head and face. Also known as a caul, this strange and rare occurrence appears in only one out of every 80,000 births!

Mama Rosie was born with a veil over her eyes, but it really means born with a veil over your head. Mama only knows how to use the way she was born in a good way. If in her vision she sees something long before it happens and it could be harmful or danger coming to a person she will try to warn them in advance so it will not happen. She has always been dead on target on anything she foreseen.

As a little girl born in the South, I have heard the word *Born With A Veil Over Your Eyes* a lot from Mama and her siblings. Two of her sisters was born just like her and can foresee stuff and be dead on target every time just like Mama.

If Mama said to us, "Tomorrow I don't want y'all children to go the way you usually go to school I want you girls to go the long way to school, just for tomorrow."

"Why Mama?"

Her reply, "I have already seen it days earlier there is going to be a man on that corner bothering children, he walks with a limp and he will have a red shirt on." If she sees it before it happens, she is always dead on target.

Because me and sisters knows she was born with the veil over her head and can see things long before it happen we always do what she said.

The way Mom was born she only knew how to make her gift work to stop danger or harm from coming to another person. You might be a person she does not know that well, it did not matter. If she foresee something bad coming that will affect your life she will warn you in a heartbeat. If Mom calls it that is the way it is going to happen.

Buttermilk and Cornbread

Our mother loved buttermilk and cooked cornbread mixed together in a glass. She would sit at our dinner table with a big glass of buttermilk, break the cornbread up in the glass, stir it and start eating out of the glass with a spoon. After she let the first teaspoonful go down her throat, a facial expression came over her face as if it was the best food she has ever eaten.

As a little girl sitting at the table watching her eat the glass of buttermilk with the cornbread, I wanted some. With the happy face she made while eating it I thought it must be some good eating.

I go into the kitchen to get me a glass of buttermilk and a piece of cornbread. Sat back at our dinner table with Mama—mix my cornbread into the glass of buttermilk, just like Mama. When I put a spoonful into my mouth, I thought it tasted horrible. I do not like wet bread and never ate any buttermilk and cornbread after that.

Leaving the South in the late 1940's, at the age of five years old, growing up in Los Angeles I have never seen any of my friends eating buttermilk with cornbread mixed in a glass. It must be a southern thing.

Cleanliness Is Next To Godliness

Definition, It is important to be clean as it is to be good.

Our mother Rosie was the cleanest person. She kept her house spotless 24/7. If you walked into her house and was a dirty person or a musty person, she would react. She would point blank tell them, "Child, you can't sit on my couch." Go and get them a card table chair which was either made out of metal or wood and have them sit on it. She will respond the same way if you are a person who does not take a bath and she can smell your funk. The first words out of her mouth would go like this, "Child you are stinking and you need to do something about yourself."

Do not knock at her door with any type of illness, such as coughing and sounding like you have the flu. If you do Mama will step back and leave just a little opening in the door to talk. The first thing out of her mouth, "Child you cannot come in here I catch everything." Say goodbye and close the door. I'd better say it the way Mama says it, "I will catch every thang."

Heaven help you if she gets on an elevator with you and you are coughing and sneezing and not cover your mouth and nose with your hands or a handkerchief. She does not care that you are a total stranger—she will move as far away from you as possible and the first words out of her mouth, "Child you need to put something over your mouth and nose I catch everything. There is no shame in her game, if it is for right.

Mama's Hip Dance–1925

In 1925 when Mom was five years old, she and her older sister, Aunt Mary (Sang), would spend the weekend and stay overnight at their sister's house in Benton, Louisiana, Aunt Cora (Bit), which was not far from Cotton Valley.

On a Saturday they all would go to the big city of Shreveport, Louisiana to a place they called 'The Levee. Aunt Sang had this big tin cup, sit it on the grown so people would put money in it while Mama did her singing and dancing act. The crowd would gather around watching Mama perform her Hip Dance and Singing act, throwing money into the tin can on the ground. Every time the can got full of coins and dollars, Aunt Sang would dump the can in a bag.

Mama was born knowing how to do all the gymnastic and acrobatic moves without being trained, she was born like that.

One day I asked Mama, "How does the Hip Dance go?" She said, "Baby, you stand up and go all the way back with your hands and touch the ground and then come up dancing with your hips moving them real fast side to side and just work those hips."

Can you imagine a five year old doing her singing and dancing act as if she was an adult who had professional training. Mama said when she got back home down in those woods she had so much money.

Aunt Sang, her oldest sister decided they needed a larger container to hold all the money Mama made doing her act. Aunt Sang started taking with them one of the church money basket you'd take up a collection in because it held more money where she would not have to keep dumping the tin can into the bag.

When Mama became about nineteen years old she said she would go into her town of Cotton Valley at the railroad station where all the World War II soldiers were boarding the train to go off to war. She would start doing her singing and dancing act and the soldiers and everybody standing around her would put all their money into the church collection basket she had on the ground.

When the train pulled off with the World War II soldiers in it, Mama said the guys would stick their hands out of the window as if they wanted to grab her and said, "Baby come go with us." Mama said, "I told them they can look but can't touch I came here to sing and dance and that is all I came here for. Ethel Mae, you know your Mama had to tell them as fine as I was with that pretty shaped figure."

My reply, "I know you did Miss Fine."

Mama Goes to Jail–1933

Our mom Rosie was arrested in 1933 at the age of thirteen years old, but not for a crime. She spent two hours in jail.

Grandma Virginia expired in 1933 when Mama was thirteen years old. Mama said she talked her first cousin Nora into letting her tag alone with her to this little juke joint in the woods, cousin Nora was grown and Mama wasn't.

Mama waited until her father had gone to sleep so she could sneak out of the house. Mama said she felt like dancing and partying. She said she was having a ball on the dance floor.

When they got ready to leave the juke joint and go, Mama had to pee, but the outhouse was behind the juke joint. Mama said she was scared to go back there because she thought she might step on a snake. Instead she went on the side of the juke joint to urinate. She pulled down her panties and squat and that is when she said the old white sheriff walked up on them shining his flash light on her. She said, "That old sheriff was trying to shine that flash light underneath my dress and I told him if you see something your grandmammy ain't got, throw in your hat." The old sheriff lets Cousin Nora, the adult, go home but he takes my thirteen year old Mama Rosie Lee to jail in town.

Cousin Nora goes home, back the woods, and

rumor spreads. “Old sheriff done arrested Rosie Lee.”

Word gets to Mom's older brother Uncle Jethro (Buddy), born 1901 and is nineteen years older than her. Uncle Buddy, the minister, hitch up his horse and wagon to go into town to get her out of jail. Mama said she did not know he had a switch with him until she climbed into the wagon.

He took the switch and whacked her a couple of times across her legs and said, "You ain't nothing but a disgrace to the family."

Mama said, "Ethel Mae that old Buddy made me sick."

In those days in the woods where our family lived, on both sides, there were no bathrooms, running water, or electricity. They had an outhouse, smokehouse, mule, horse and other animals. Grandpa Charles could not read or write, but he could tell time by listening to his rooster crow and by looking up at the sky and sun. Mama said Grandma Virginia could read, write and knew her numbers. Mama said their plantation owner Old Man Hayes wife taught grandma all of her book education. Listening to Mama, everybody in the county loved her family.

Study shows the rooster does not need the light of a new day to know when it is down—rather their internal clocks alert them to the time.

When I got a little older than five years old, if the

family did not have clocks, I thought to myself what if the rooster was sick and cannot crow how would Grandpa tell the time. I forgot to ask Daddy and Mama how that was done, leaving the South at such an early age of five years old, in the late 1940's.

Rosie Lee Walker's First Husband 1935

In 1935 Mama married her first husband Grant who was seven years older than her. She said she did not love him, but her father was so strict it made her want to leave home. She said she wanted a man that treat her right and had a job. Grant came alone and convinced Grandpa and Mama he was the right man for her, so they thought and Grant and Mama got married. They never had any children together.

The next day after they were married was the first time she found out he was crazy and jealous. Mama said on the second day they were married he had to go into town and when he got ready to leave the house he grabbed a broom and went outside and started walking backwards sweeping his foot prints so he would be able to tell if a man had come over while he was gone. Mama said, "The fool married the wrong fifteen year old." She said she got a pair of his shoes and a pair of her high heels walked outside and started pressing them hard into the dirt in just the right spot so it would look like a man had been there. When he got home Mama said he was acting real strange but did not say a single word to her.

The next day when he got ready to leave the house Mama said he got a hammer and some nails, walked out the door and started nailing up the door and all the windows so she could not get out until he got back. Mama said there was an ax in the house and a rifle over the fire place. She said she grabbed the ax and started chopping at the door until it came loose. She said she went over to the fire place and grabbed the rifle, loaded it and ran as fast as she could down the dirt road until she caught up with him. She said, "Do you remember the weekly TV series that use to come on TV called 'The Rifle Man? I was firing those bullets out that rifle at his feet just as fast as I could making him dance down the dirt road and I would reload firing again making him dance down the road. I could have killed him if I wanted, but I did not want to kill him."

When he got to the creek he fell backwards into the water. She said, "I fired a couple of shots to the right of him and a couple to the left making sure I did not hit him. I went into our little shot gun house and packed my suitcase and went back home to my Papa. I was only married to that fool three days."

Mama said Grandpa told her she could handle a gun and knife was well as any man since she was a little girl. Mama is the sweetest person but do not bring any mess to her because you are not going to win, I don't care how big and tall you are. She said, "Back in the day the big ones was easier for me to knock out then the little ones, more meat baby."

Even though Grant and my Mama split up after three days, Mama said they never got a divorce. She said he was so sad about losing her it made him join the army and sent off overseas to World War II. Mama said he was so crazy and did not die from combat like some of the other soldiers but instead he made his own Military Police (MPs) shoot and kill him.

Mama said when she got the papers explaining his death she could believe it because he was that crazy. Mama said, *"That fool was as crazy as fifty-two asses."* Our mother was referring to donkeys and mules, she does not curse.

Mama Could Dance The Jitterbug The 1940s

Daddy said Mama was the best dancer ever from the 1920's through the 1980's, and I agree. She had no professional training but could out dance anyone. The only two people who could beat her dancing were The Famous Tap Dancing/Actor Nicholas Brothers, one of the Nicholas brothers married Mrs. Dorothy Dandridge when she was eighteen years old. I thought Mrs. Dandridge was so pretty in person and on the big movie screen

Daddy said Mama was very competitive, and do not get on the dance floor with her because she would hang you out to dry, making a person walk off the dance floor tired and shaking their heads while she was still out there doing her thing.

When she did the Jitterbug with her partner, I don't care how tall he was, she could leap over his head and he could swing her straight through his legs and with perfect timing she would land on her feet as if she had wings

No matter how poor everybody was in those 1800's through the 1900's in the south when they went to church or stepped out to party, they dressed as sharp as a tack, hat and all. Some of the poor ones in that era could sew and made their own clothes. Back in those days everything was a better quality—things were made in America.

Our grandparents, on both sides, and all their children were very clean. Some might have had to make their own soap but were cleaner than a lot of people now who buy things already made.

Our father and mom were the sharpest dressers ever. When they stepped out, it had to be laid from head to toe.

Daddy Shipped Off Overseas To World War II—1942

Before our father Hanspard Walker was shipped off oversees to fight in World War II, our mother, Rosie Lee, gave birth to their first born which was a girl named Ethel Mae. He was there for my birth. But when it was time for Mama to give birth to their second daughter Juanita, Dad was already oversees fighting the war against our enemies and was not there for her like he was for me.

Grandpa Charles was like a father to Juanita and I while Daddy was overseas. Sometimes when he was not working his crop out in the fields–if he had to go into our town he would take me and Juanita with him. He would hitch up his horse and wagon, put Juanita and I into the wagon and we would leave out of the woods and go into our little town of Cotton Valley, I was less than five years old. When he parked the wagon he would always say it twice to me and Juanita, while we were in the wagon and then repeated the same thing when he lifted us down to the ground.

"If a white person is walking toward you or you are passing them, you children must not look them in the face and always look down at the ground."

The way he said –it sounded as if it was a bad

thing to do or something terrible might happen to you. If I looked at a white person in the face, did it mean I would be killed or turned to salt? Heck, I was just a little girl, the way he said it that is what it sounded like to me.

After Daddy was discharged from World War II in 1947 and we moved to Los Angeles it was okay to look a white person or any other race in the face. I sure was glad Daddy and Mama bought us out of those woods down south. Being lynched just for looking a white person in the face did not seem like a crime to me.

Mt. Sariah Baptist Church Cotton Valley, Louisiana

Mt. Sariah Baptist Church, in Cotton Valley, Louisiana is about one hundred and forty-two years old. It has been there since about 1874.

Our grandparents, parents, and family on both sides attended Mt. Sariah Baptist Church. Daddy and Mama grew up in this church. Mom's oldest brother, Pastor Jethro Edwards (Buddy), born in 1901, was a pastor at this church.

In 2005, my husband's family had a Family Reunion in Shreveport, Louisiana. While visiting his family I decided to drive to Cotton Valley to visit my family, on both sides. The distance between Shreveport, Louisiana and Cotton Valley, Louisiana is about fifty miles.

While visiting my family in Cotton Valley I stayed with Aunt Mut, my father's sister who was born in 1922. A few of my cousins told me Mt. Sariah Baptist church had been torn down and remodeled. We drove over to the church, which was not more than five minutes, by car. When we drove up I could not believe my eyes. It was a church built out of the most beautiful bricks and looked so modern. When I walked inside the church, it was large and elegant, and the decor was off the chain. I only remember the little wood church that Daddy and Mama grew up in.

All around the top of the walls were photos in a picture frame of all the pastors who ministered at the church since the late 1880's. Mom's brother, Pastor Jethro Edwards (Buddy) photo was at the top of wall with the other pastors.

The Family Move From Louisiana To Los Angeles—1947

In 1947 our father, Hanspard Walker (Hamp), a World a War II–Veteran and our Mom Rosie Lee Walker decided to move to Los Angeles, California bringing with them their two daughters,

Ethel Mae and Juanita. Daddy thought it would be a better life for a black male and more opportunities than it was in the south. Daddy was what one would call "a genius." I do not care what your chosen profession you mastered if it was something Daddy did not know or was trained in—after you taught him he would master it and be able to teach you more than you knew. Because of his creative, inventive, and genius mind he would take learning to another level.

When we arrived in Los Angeles from the South, Mama was pregnant with her third child who was in the oven waiting to be born the first kid in a big city. The other two daughters were born years later.

We lived on 33rd Street in Los Angeles which was between the streets of Stanford and Griffith. The side of town we lived on in those days was called, 'The East Side.' When we walked into the house I thought I had died and gone to heaven. At the age of five years old was the first time I saw a knob where hot and cold water ran out. I called them knobs because I had never seen a faucet. Daddy turned one faucet and then the other. Hot water came out of one and cold water came out the other. Daddy and Mama said when I saw the water coming out of the faucet my eyes got so big.

They walked into what was called a bathroom—in the bathroom was what they called a toilet. The toilet was seated on the floor with the back to the wall. The toilet tank was mounted to the ceiling with the back of it leveled to the wall. Pipes ran down the wall from the back of the toilet tank to the toilet seated on the floor. Underneath the toilet tank was a long chain. If you pulled the chain the water would go out of the toilet which was seated on the floor. Mama said I thought it was going into the back yard and the back yard would be stinky.

We two little girls, Ethel Mae and Juanita, will always thank God, Daddy and Mama for bringing us out of those woods down South before we were old enough to pick all those bales of cotton. We have never hated anything but I bet we would have hated picking cotton.

When I got a little older than five years old I thought the children in California were lazy. They had a toilet that flushed and running water. The boys were complaining about cutting the lawn and had a lawn mower. They did not have to hitch up a mule and plow acres of land. The girls were complaining about washing the dishes. They had hot and cold running water and did not have to go to a well or creek to get the water. When I got a little older I realized my friends were not lazy that was all they knew.

In the southern town we lived, we had an outhouse, smokehouse, well, mule, horse and wagon, and the pee pot was placed by our bed at night. When it was time for me and Juanita to be bathed we were placed into a big round tin pan. The water was heated on top of the stove and poured into the tin pan we bathed in.

Our father found his first job within two weeks after we arrived in Los Angeles in 1947. He found a job as a chauffeur for this rich white family in Beverly Hills. Daddy said he worked for them only one month because the wife was a racist person. One day she had Daddy chauffeur her around to do her shopping, when he pulled up to the stop light the lady said, "Nigger, pull this car over in front of that store." Daddy said he did not say a word—stepped out the car and left it in the middle of the street at a stop light. He walked to the nearest bus stop and went home.

The lady's husband liked Daddy a lot and thought he was a very good worker. Daddy said the guy called him on the phone because he wanted him to come back and work for him, but he told him no and what his wife called him. He explained to his ex-boss people who are like her was the reason he left the south. Daddy said the guy apologized for her.

Daddy went back to school to complete his education while working on his second job. After that he went off into construction work framing houses and until he retired. With wood his work was like a Picasso painting. He could make anything out of wood.

Mama told us when they were children he could

pick up a piece of wood, get his knife, start carving away at the wood and make an image of anything out of wood, including how a person looked.

Our parents and uncles bought a little of the South with them to Los Angeles. We had a big garden planted in our back yard, a chicken coup and chickens. We can remember mama going out to feed the chickens and a few of her daughters would join in throwing the food to them. We enjoyed watching her gather the eggs from the chicken coup. We had no washer and washer, clothes were done on a scrub board. Mama would pass a small garment to her youngest daughter to scrub so she could think she was doing something.

Mama never learned how to drive a car and especially after she was hit by a car on her way to the neighborhood pharmacy, but she sure could get from one point to the other without a car.

Food was bought to your door. We had Helm's Bakery that would come in front of our house; that is where we got fresh bread, fresh donuts, and cookies. We had the milkman who would deliver fresh milk in a bottle to our front door. We had the Fishman who came with fresh fish and he had a scale to weigh the fish. We had the Good Humor ice cream man that had all different flavors of ice cream and popsicles. It would be very benefitting to some children today if they experience what they call the primitive times. We enjoyed watching mom choose the vegetables from the vegetable truck. The stores would come to us.

We can recall mama taking in hobo's which is called homeless now a days, feeding them a little something and giving them some clean cloths but our dad and both of our uncles put a stop to that because one evening one of the hobo's while at the dinner table pulled a weapon out and robbed the men.

We can recall mama taking in an elderly woman and we enjoyed that because our Dad's mother was still in the South and mom's mother had passed away when mom was thirteen and it felt good to have someone around us in our state we could consider as a grandmother. The elderly lady was bed stricken and come to find out Granny was drunk. Mother went to turn the mattresses over and discovered Gin bottles that she had one of our uncles go buy it for her and sneaked it to her. Well out went Granny.

As children growing up on 33rd Street in Los Angeles, children would come and sit on the porch around our mother and listen to the stories she would tell. The adults all knew one another and in the summer everyone would sit out on their porches while we kids played ball in the streets and we had neighborhood police that knew who every one of us kids parents were.

As children in the 1940's through the 1960's, we

were raised in an old-fashioned Southern way by our parents. Giving respect to all adults was a given. We, as children thought talking back or cursing your parents was one of the biggest sins other than murder. We really believed if you talk back or curse your parents a bolt of lightning would strike you down.

We arrived in Los Angeles in 1947 just in time for me to start my first year of kindergarten. My elementary school was 28th Street Elementary School, 2807 Stanford Ave., Los Angeles, CA 90011.

In my kindergarten class was all races, Blacks, Whites, Jewish, Japanese, Chinese, but only one Latino and he became a medical doctor. My one little Latino friend in my class, his father owned a shoe store one block from our house. Sometimes Mama would take our shoes to the shoe shop to have taps put on the soles. Most of the children parents did the same thing. They thought the taps on the heel of the shoe would make the shoe last longer.

Some teachers would give us homework on a subject they taught for the week. Sometimes their teaching was all drawn out in a complicated way which you did not understand quite well. Daddy would have me give him my homework, go over to the kitchen table, sit down a while and study over it. When he got up from the table he had figure out a way to make the subject quick, easier and made it fun.

Daddy walked over to me and said, "Ethel Mae, there is an easier way to figure out this problem your teacher showed you how to do."

Whatever he did at the table going over my homework, it worked and was easily learned at the snap of a finger. If there was a test given, I'd ace the test because of the fun and easy way Daddy taught me.

"Daddy, you should ask the principal if you could come to school and teach the other teachers your fun–way and it is going to make the kids want to learn."

"No baby, I will just teach my children and grandchildren."

Daddy was a genius on anything a person found difficult to learn. With his creative mine he knew how to turn something difficult into simplicity and fun where a first grader could understand it.

Mr. Kelly, Juanita's 4th grade teacher at 28th Street School in Los Angeles, took her 4th grade class on a field trip to the Bank of America which was not more than one block from the school and he showed the class how to open up a savings account. He was teaching them how to save money.

Our father, uncle, and their friends played dominoes almost every day. Daddy cut a hole in a cigar box and when his friends arrived, Juanita would station herself on a chair at the front door holding the cigar box and Daddy's friends would drop a quarter inside. But some thought she was so cute, they would give her a dollar. Juanita would make them sandwiches, and bring them ice water and Kool-Aid. She also baby sit and sold Christmas cards. By the time she was nineteen years old, she had enough money saved to pay for her entire wedding. She was born just as lucky as Mama. With her and Mama it would not surprise me if an airplane flew over their heads and one million dollars dropped on top of their heads.

Massive Tornado Hits Cotton Valley, Louisiana–1947

18 Killed and 200 Injured

In 1947 after we arrived in Los Angeles from Louisiana Daddy and Mama gets this call that a massive tornado had hit our town in Cotton Valley, Louisiana and some people were killed and hundreds injured. But none of our family was killed.

New Year's Day, 1947, a massive tornado struck our town of Cotton Valley. Mama said it practically destroyed it. Eighteen people were killed and two hundred injured. But the tornado only hit in the town of Cotton Valley not back in the woods where most of our family lived on both sides.

Aunt Sang's husband, Uncle Willie Jackson,

World War I Veteran, was blown out of their house. He broke his legs but ended up okay. They lived in the city of Cotton Valley not back in the woods.

Cotton Valley reminds me of a movie I saw on TV called 'Rosewood' and also of a book I read called 'Black Wall Street' except for the riots and massacres that took place, that never happened in our town of Cotton Valley, Louisiana.

Like in the books of Rosewood and Black Wall Street, Cotton Valley in our Mom's era was a booming town. Our town had everything, oil was discovered, big theaters, stores, banks, and its own train station where you did not have to go all the way to Minden or Shreveport to catch a train. After the tornado hit in 1947 and destroyed our little town, it was never the same as it was when our grandparents and parents lived there.

Aunt Sang and Mama had more ways alike than their other siblings, both knew how to make money and both were very lucky. It would not surprise me, with their luck, if one or the other walked out the door and step on a $500 dollar bill on the sidewalk and repeated the same thing on another street the following week. Both never had to beg or steal, but they always had fine clothes and money.

People would give them money who would not give it to anyone else. They are the only two women I know who can go to any big affair penniless and leave with $200 dollars or more. They will walk over to any relative and stick out their hands, rub all their fingers together on one hand and say, "Baby let Auntie hold something." The person would go into their pockets and give them all these dollars. If I did not know any better you would have thought they hypnotized the person, but they didn't. Whatever magic they had the people gave them money, and reacted as if that was the best move they had ever made.

Mr. and Mrs. I Spy

When we were children in the 1940's through the 1950's we played outside with all the other children and we had so much fun, but don't let night catch you or you would be in big trouble.

One time night caught me and my sister Juanita. I could see Mama walking down the street looking for us as we were trying to get home. I took off running past Mama headed for the house. When I got into the house I locked myself into the bathroom and wouldn't come out.

I could hear Mama's voice through the door, "Ethel Mae, Gal open up this door."

"No Mama, you told us not to let night catch us."

"Gal, I ain't going to do nothing to you bring your behind out."

I opened the door and came out, and she hugged me. My sister Juanita said she didn't think anything about it, and walked side by side with Mama all the way home, but not me.

All adults in the neighborhood watched out for every child. If you did one thing wrong, by the time you got into the house from playing your Daddy and Mama already found out. I'd say, "How did they find out that quick, it must been Mr. and Mrs. I Spy who told them. They made me sick trying to get all into my business." Like at nine years old I had a lot of business for them to get in. I use to think they must have sent up smoke signals to each other to find out so fast. Just as soon as I became an adult I changed that tune to thank *God* for all of the Mr. and Mrs. I Spy folks.

Growing Up In Los Angeles In The 1940s–1950s

As a child I did not like visiting down south when school was out. The idea of leaving hot and cold running water and a bathroom with a toilet that flushed was a terrible thought. I did not think I was asking for too much. I was scared of going to an outhouse because I thought I might step on a snake and I hate snakes. After a few visits, I had hoped Daddy and Mama would send money back to our grandparents in Louisiana to come here. I knew once they arrived in Los Angeles they were going to love the hot and cold running water and a bathroom with a toilet that flushed.

Daddy said, "I don't care how high on the hog you girls get remember your roots, be yourself, and act down to earth." If I was a gambler, which I'm not, I would take Daddy and Mama to Las Vegas put both of them on top of a gambling table and say let it ride until my voice was gone. Both are what one would call "a sure bet."

No matter what they have told us in our life they have always been on target. Unbelievable! I can think of a few things I've told my children when they were growing up, that I thought was right but I was wrong. I wonder how Daddy and Mama were so dead on target every time.

Leaving Your Food or Drink—Take it With You

Mama always taught us if we were eating or drinking out of a glass or a cup and had to leave the table—unless our grandparents or parents are at the table to watch our food and drink while we were gone, when we returned it is no longer ours. She always thought an evil person would put something in your food or drink if you left it at the table and did not take it with you.

Some years later, after I started high school, my friends and I were sitting at one of the tables outside for students to eat. At the next table sitting was a boy and girl – I did not personally know them. I had seen them around the campus. The girl got up and left the table and left her drink in a cup on the table. Just as soon as the boy saw her leave he went into his shirt pocket and pulled out a little plastic bag with something that looked like a white powder. He dumped it into the girl's cup.

We teenagers did not know what to do because we did not want her to drink out of her cup when she returned. I said to my best girlfriend seated next to me "I am going to go past the table and knock over her cup, and pretend to the boy it was an accident." I pulled it off successfully and apologized to the boy for being so clumsy. I was not a bit sorry.

When I got home I told Daddy about what had happened at school about the boy and the girl. I found out the boy and the girl's name before I left school. Daddy reported my story to the Principal the next day. I don't know what happened but after that I never saw the boy or girl together again the entire time I was at school.

Daddy's BBQ & Domino Playing

Every day except Sunday, the men would come over to our house to play dominoes with Daddy. Daddy was very competitive and rarely lost a domino game. When he sat at the table with his opponents he took the game very serious. Do not be his partner and make a dumb play because if you do you will hear and see him demonstrate a bad attitude. Daddy had the ability to know the next play his opponent would make before he made it. Daddy always whistled when he played dominoes and barbecued.

Mama was the best cook—but our World War II father made the best barbecue on his pits in his back yard. Daddy was very creative with his hands and could make anything. He got two big black barrels, cut and measured them and when he finished they looked custom made.

Daddy needed two large pits. People from all over paid him any price he asked to cook barbecue for them, but he always gave them a fair price and did not over charge.

Daddy's barbecue was so good you did not need any barbecue sauce. The first bite you took was so good it made you want to chew the bone and suck all of the juice out, just like a dog.

Growing up my sisters and I would go into the kitchen and watch Mama cook, trying to learn the good–cooking lady's techniques. Daddy and Mom's third daughter was the only daughter who hung out in the back yard with Daddy, we call her Lil Mama. She would watch his every move on how he prepared his meat, cooked it and make his homemade barbecue sauce. Today, Lil Mama is the daughter out of the five who has Dad's barbecue technique down pat, not his other daughters.

Mama's cooking was so good it made you want to lick every single thing off of the plate with your tongue and make the plate look like it was washed in dish water and soap. Her food is what you would call 'licking good— and yes it will make you want to hurt yourself.

Central Avenue in Los Angeles 1920s–1950s

Our house was five minutes from 33rd and Central Avenue by car. Sometimes if one of the great entertainers were in town and was going to perform at one of the nightclubs or one of the theatres on Central Avenue, Daddy and Mama would dress to kill to go see them perform. They are the ones their daughters got that dress-to-kill from. In the 1920-1960s people dressed.

Central Avenue was like Disneyland. Everybody wanted to visit Central Avenue from all over the world. Up and down Central Avenue were all races of businesses—Black, Jewish, Asian, and Caucasian. There were so many black-owned businesses in this era. Practically every black who migrated from the south bought and owned a home.

Many men after they were discharged from World War II, such as our father, within two weeks after their arrival in Los Angeles found a job. Jobs were plentiful in California during the 1940s through the 1960s. The population was very low. It would not have been unusual to find two to three different jobs, the same day.

The Lincoln Theatre–1950s

Over A 900 Seat Theatre

You had the Lincoln Theatre and Bill Robinson theatre, named after Bill 'Bojangles' Robinson born 1878. He was a famous black tap dancer and actor in movies from the 1930s through the 1940s. Some of you might have seen Mr. Bojangles in old movies tap dancing with the most famous child movie star in the world, at the time. The little girl was Shirley Temple.

The Lincoln Theatre was located at 2300 South Central Avenue, Los Angeles, California. The Lincoln Theatre opened in 1926 and became the largest venue for black entertainment on the West Coast.

As one of the first theatres in the country and Southern California for African American audiences, the Lincoln featured motions pictures, live stage shows, talent shows and vaudeville, earning critical acclaim as the 'West Coast Apollo. Bardu Ali's band served as a master of ceremonies for the Lincoln Theatre. Noted performers at the Lincoln theatre included Count Basie, Duke Ellington, Bill 'Bojangles' Robinson, Lionel Hampton, Cab Calloway, Lena Horne, Nat King Cole and the list goes on.

Sunday stage attractions at the Lincoln Theatre cost thirty cents for adults and ten cents for children. The Lincoln Theatre competed for business with other local venues including the Bill Robinson Theatre at 4319 Central Ave., the Florence Mills Theatre at 3511 Central Ave., the Hub Theatre at 1007 Central Ave, the Rosebud Theatre at 1940 Central Ave., and the Savoy Theatre at 5326 Central Avenue.

For almost a year after it opened, The Lincoln Theatre was the only entertainment available to blacks in a racially segregated environment. Lincoln Theatre's popularity was even felt by Central Ave. nightclub owners who reported a slumping year in 1927.

In 1952, my sister Juanita was only nine years old when she won the talent show at the Lincoln Theatre. She always could sing and dance like our mother, both knew how to work an audience at a very early age. The talent shows at the Lincoln Theatre was supposed to be for adults only but my little nine year old sister with her persuasive power like our mother talked the guy into letting her try out and perform on the stage with the adults.

Juanita sang a song by Ruth Brown called "Mama You Treat Your Daughter Mean" and tore it up and got a standing ovation. She said she was so little and did not know what the words to the song meant other than the song had a good beat and sound.

The little nine year old girl beat out all the adults and won $30. In 1952, $30 was like winning $300. A working man did not make that much money in a week not in those days. Juanita always did know how to make her some money and she was nothing but a little nine year old girl.

Burning Hair and Underwear In the Incinerator—1950s

In the late 1940's, when we arrived in Los Angeles from Louisiana, everybody had an incinerator in their back yard. Homeowners and landlords had been allowed to burn their rubbish in the incinerator since the turn of the century. Because of all the pollution by the incinerator a total ban on incinerators was placed October 1, 1957.

It used to be fun to take out the trash, fill that puppy full and throw it into the incinerator in the back yard, light a match and throw it in.

Mama had two things she would not let leave her sight without making sure she personally burned it in our incinerator in the back yard and that was our underwear we had outgrown and any of our hair she cut. She would not mix it in with other trash, but burn it separate.

Daddy and Mom's family down south believed if someone gets your hair or underwear and was an evil person, they knew how to make a person's life miserable if they did not like you. Mama and her family calls it 'hoodoo, but the real terminology is 'voodoo. Mama said it might be true or false she was not taking a chance when it came to her children.

In the Los Angeles Unified School District, religion being taught in the schools was a given. If you did not want your children to be taught religion in elementary school K-6, you would have to take them out and place them in a private school.

I forget how often we were dismissed out of our classroom and sent out to the school yard to different bungalows for our religious denomination to be taught. These were some of the different religion faiths taught in each bungalow, Baptist, Catholic, Jewish, and Buddhism.

When we arrived in Los Angeles in 1947 after Daddy was discharged from World War II, none of the white people would let any Japanese move into their neighborhood including my little five year old kindergarten Japanese friends. They held everybody responsible for the bombing of Pearl Harbor. Mama said I did not like that because they were only five years old like me. I could not understand why anyone would hate a five year old for something an adult had done.

The population in California was not large and in my elementary kindergarten class there might have been ten to twelve students. With such few students it was as if you were in a private school where the teacher had the time to give each student their individual time. That was the way it was in my elementary school in Los Angeles in the 40's.

My sister Juanita, who is one year seven months younger than me, I knew the following year it would be her time to enter kindergarten. I gave her a few tips on what I had learned so she would be ready when she got there. Even though she is very smart I thought it might help.

In my day the Los Angeles Unified School District went like this, Elementary school K-6th grade, Junior High School 7th-9th grade, and High School 10th -12th grade. When you graduated from any of the three you had to dress up for the graduation ceremony.

In the 1940s through the 1960s all schools had rules and regulations and I thought some of them were a little too strict. In Junior High School, grades seven through the ninth, if a girl wore nylons she would get suspended from school. In high school a girl could not ware an engagement ring because you would get in trouble.

I've seen a few classmates clown in class. The teacher would make arrangements with their parents and the parent would do a surprise visit to the class and would sit through the entire class at a desk. You do not want to act up and your parents get a call from your teacher. I know I did not want such a thing to happen to me because getting embarrassed in front of your classmates is not a good thing.

As children, if we did get mad at anything our parents said—we had better zip it up, go into our bedroom, close the door and tell off the air quietly. You don't want to tell the air off too loud because you did not want it to go through the door and your parents heard you. I feared consequence. For me it is what do you want and when do you want it Daddy and Mama.

Coca-Cola Building

1334 So. Central Ave. Los Angeles, Ca.

Built in the 1930s and declared a city cultural landmark in 1976, this plant is still bottling Coca-Cola today

Many young people took their first driving lessons on the lot of the Coca-Cola Factory on the weekends when the employees were off. I was one of those people at the age of twelve. I was too young to get my driver license but Daddy always prepared us years in advance for everything.

Daddy had an old 1948 stick shift Ford Coupe, a pretty car. Back–in–the day cars were made out of steel, unlike now, and the curves on the body of the car was awesome. We got into the car and drove down to the Coca Cola Factory lot. After we arrived I took out my scratch paper and started writing down everything Daddy was telling me how to do. I bought with me a pillow because I was too short. Daddy and I switched seats placing me in the driver's seat at the steering wheel.

He taught me to drive a car as if he was teaching me how to drive a big rig truck with only my right and left door mirrors as my guide to see. It is as if I can hear Daddy's voice now, "Ethel Mae, press the clutch all the way down to the floor, and don't strip Daddy's gear."

When I first sat behind the steering wheel Daddy

had me practice looking out of the front window and turning my head very little to look out of the left front and right door mirror on each door. He was teaching me a method of seeing as much as I could of the entire perimeter of the car at one time. He said if I was parallel parking on the right curve and turn my head all the way around to the back, I would not be able to see anything that was coming at my car from the front.

After Daddy taught me how to drive you could have put a cardboard box over the entire back window, I would have been able to parallel park my car from the right or do anything on the left because he taught me how to use both mirrors on both doors.

At age sixteen when I went to get my driver license at the DMV on Jefferson and Grand in Los Angeles, if I did not have a mirror on my right car door I would have failed on the parallel parking because I only knew how to parallel park using my right door mirror. To this day I do not like driving a car that does not have the right mirror on the right door.

Many years later on the 5 North Freeway, leaving Orange County, a big object flew off the truck and hit and cracked my front window. With my eyes on the front I saw it coming and ducked.

My first baby who was born in 1961 was in the front seat next to me wrapped in a blanket. He rolled off the seat onto the floor. I was stretching and reaching my body and hands as far as I could to get him back into the seat, but I never took my eyes off of the front window to look out. Because of Daddy's teaching me how to drive at the age of twelve years old, it taught me that it only takes a second for your eyes to be off the road for a possible fatal accident to occur.

Racism Experienced For the First Time In Los Angeles–1952

Growing up in Los Angeles, I only experienced racism twice. My fifth grade elementary teacher and my tenth grade science teacher.

In 1952 we moved to 59th and Broadway in Los Angeles just in time for me to start the fifth grade. It was an all-white neighborhood and an all-white elementary school. I was in the fifth grade, my sister Juanita was in the fourth grade, and my baby sister was in kindergarten and the other two sisters were not born yet. In those days kindergarten let out at 11,30 a.m. and the upper grades at 3:00 p.m.

I was an 'A' student in my classroom of all whites. One day the teacher asked me to stay after class, and dismissed all the white children. While seated at my desk she wanted to know if there was any white blood in my family. I told her yes, Grandma Virginia has white and Indian blood in her. To this day I cannot remember if she said, I knew it or I thought so because you are just too smart. I tell you one thing this little fifth grade did not know what she meant and thought it was a stupid question.

I said I will wait until Daddy get home from work and ask him what the teacher meant by the question. There was no way I was going to tell Mama what happened because if she found out the teacher kept me after school over some racist stuff she was not going to be a very nice person. When it comes to negative stuff being placed up on her children she will take it to another level.

Until Daddy explained to me what she meant is when I understood why she asked me such a stupid question. As if a black person cannot have a brain unless they have one drop of white blood running through their veins. Wrong! I was glad to graduate from the sixth grade at this school.

When I arrived at Junior High School, in my 7th grade Algebra class a set of twins from Africa checked into my class. They were the smartest students I have personally known, geniuses. They were the type of students who would forget to open their book and be surprised they got an 'A.' I can pull an 'A' off, but I have to open the book to know what is in it. You have no idea how happy I was the twins from Africa was so smart, not one drop of white blood in their veins from slavery days hundreds of years earlier. It only proved Daddy was right in the first place.

Virginia Marie Walker Jones 1952–1982

Rosie Walker's Fourth Daughter

In 1952, Mama gave birth to her fourth daughter, Virginia Marie. She was a pretty chocolate girl. She got her skin color from Mama's father who we called Grandpa Charles (1874-1964).

Virginia, who we all called 'Gin, could sing with a magic voice that could hold an audience attention. She loved and sang jazz. Her voice was as pretty as the recording star, Nancy Wilson but sound a little better. She was definitely a person Motown would have signed as one of their artist. Like our parents she was a sweet, brainy, and brilliant person, with a personality you would not believe. Virginia was the quiet one but don't mess with her Mom, her children, or her sisters, if you did—she would let you know where to get off.

My sisters and I can remember how she always made her children read, spell to her, and write things out. They are so smart and it carried on to Virginia's grandchildren.

I do not care what affair Virginia was invited to she would be the last to arrive. Often time when she arrived it was over, but always running and rushing faster than everybody else. You would think as fast as she was running and rushing around she would have been the first one there. Her three little children had learned to move just as fast as her, and kept up. Even though she was late, the party would start over when she arrived.

Her daughter, Tricina, who is an adult, took after her mom. Just like her Mom, she is always late to any function, but running around and rushing faster than anyone else. Everybody calls Tricina by her nickname 'Cini.

Virginia was eight years older than Mom's baby daughter Willa. You had better not look at Gin's little baby sister the wrong way, if you did it would be on like a big dog.

Virginia expired when she was twenty-nine years old and we miss her every day.

The Catholic Church–1956

Ethel Mae's First Date

The young man, who was my first date, came over our house to meet Daddy and Mama. I could not believe the way they gave him one of those FBI and CIA interrogations. I was looking up at the ceiling thinking silently to myself, "Daddy and Mama please don't embarrass me." I was surprised they did not ask for a sample of his blood before we walked out the front door.

The young man took me to visit his Catholic Church, which was not more than 10 minutes from our house by car. The church was on 33rd Street close to Central Avenue in Los Angeles. Old fashion Baptist southern raised I did not know anything about the Catholic faith. They must have gotten up and down on their knees to pray every five minutes. It was like a Junior High School gym class workout.

The priest prayed in a language I had never heard, at that time. Praying is fine but if you are going to be up and down praying every five minutes why not stay down on your knees for the entire service. In the 1950's at this church you were not coming down to any padded spot, you were either coming down to a cement floor or a solid wood floor, and on your bare knees.

I had on this little cute pink dress and dressed to kill. Messed up my dress and when I got home my knees were sore. I felt like I had been dropped out of a helicopter onto the top of a wooden bench landing on my knees and every five minutes.

Mama always sent supplies with us when we left the house. Had Mama known about the Catholic faith, she would not have let me walk out of our front door without a pillow or towel to place down on the floor to prevent me from hurting my knees.

She always believed in 'back–up stuff.

Huggy Boy and Dolphin's of Hollywood–1956

Dolphin's of Hollywood Record Shop was located on Vernon Avenue and Central, in Los Angeles. The disk jockey, Huggy Boy, arrived in Los Angeles about 1945, signed on the air over KRKD radio.

I cannot tell you how many times I use to go to this record shop to buy records from 1956-1960. I was the type of teenager if I liked a record I would play it over and over a hundred times, where eventually the record would become warped. I can hear Daddy's voice now, "Ethel Mae, if you play that record one more time Daddy might have to break it." He never broke any records.

The Bill Robinson Theatre, Los Angeles–1957

The Bill Robinson theatre was located at 4219 S. Central Ave. Los Angeles, California. Status, Closed/Demolished–Single Screen – Seats 850.

Mama said the theatre was named after Bill 'Bojangles' Robinson, birth born name Luther Robinson (1878-1949). At the age of fifteen years old, I got my first real job at the Bill Robinson Theatre. I love the fringe benefits on the popcorn, hot dogs, drinks, and candy. Unfortunate I only worked there for two weeks.

One day when it was time for me to get off from work, I picked up my purse and got me a box of popcorn to take home. As I was leaving the boss asked me to step into his office, I thought he was going to tell me something about the job. He grabbed my hand and tried to pull me down on his lap as he sat in his chair. I slapped him as hard as I could across his right jaw—picked up my purse off the floor, walked out and never looked back.

If the man had touched my body, I shall assure you I would have told my Daddy and my Mama. They would have had him on the floor crawling around trying to find his other teeth, and believe that.

Johnny Otis TV Show 1957–1963

Johnny Otis (born John Alexander Veliotes, on December 28, 1921) is an American blues, rhythm blues pianist, vibraphonist, drummer, singer, bandleader, and impresario. Otis was one of the most prominent white figures in the history of Rhythm and Blues. He was born in Vallejo, California, of Greek descent.

In 1957 Johnny Otis had a TV show which came on every week called the Johnny Otis Show. The Johnny Otis Show was on TV for six years. Otis had every great singing and recording artist on his show you can think of. Go on YouTube and watch him and Count Basie perform together.

We lived next door to three ladies by the stage name of' The Three Tons of Joy. Many times Johnny Otis would have The Three Tons of Joy_with Marie Adams appear on his TV show with their singing act. The Three Tons of Joy had a baby brother and he became my first boyfriend at age sixteen years old. In 1957 The Three Tons of Joy with Marie Adams recorded a big hit record by the name of "Mama, He's Making Eyes at Me." Often times they would sing their hit song on Johnny Otis weekly TV show.

In 1958, Johnny Otis recorded his biggest national hit record on Capitol records called 'Willie and The Hand Jive. There was a dance out called

'Hand Jive. The dance had a lot of hand movements in it. You would clap your hands and hit parts of your body to the beat of the song. To me the teen-age boys looked much better doing the 'Hand Jive than we teenager girls.

In 2006 we drove to a visiting church in Los Angeles, maybe 45 miles from my house. While in the lobby a lady walks over to me I had never seen before and said, "Hello, you don't know me but I know you and your name is Ethel and my husband and my mother-in-law have a picture of you on their table when you were a teenager."

I said, "Who is your husband?" She told me his name.

I said "My, my, my, isn't that nice of them to remember me all those years." That was what I said but here is what I was silently thinking—if Mama did not have any photos of Daddy's ex-girlfriends on their table why would their five daughters.

The Surprise Baby–1959

In 1959 Mama Rosie had a surprise baby named Willa. I was in the twelfth grade. Mama was feeling a little funny about the body, but she did not know what it was. She decided to go see the doctor. The doctor told her she was pregnant. Mama would not believe the doctor. She looked at the doctor and said, "Oh no, somebody is going to tell me something, I cannot be pregnant my oldest daughter is in the twelfth grade."

Because she did not believe the first doctor, she paid $30 to go a second doctor. She would not believe the second doctor either. She goes to a third doctor and paid another $30, he told her the same thing that she was pregnant. None of the three doctors knew she was going to the other. After wasting all of her different $30 dollars she finally believed she was pregnant.

Having a surprise baby many years after the older children—parents raise the child completely different than they did their older children. They spoil the child and let them get away with more stuff. Everybody spoiled Willa. Mama let her suck a baby bottle until she was in kindergarten. Before Willa left home to go to her kindergarten, Mama would fill the baby bottle with a little milk for her to suck before Mom took her to school. When she got out of school, Mom would put a little more milk in her bottle for her to suck. Mama said she did not care just so long as her baby did not cry. She was like a little baby doll to her older sisters, a few of us are old enough to be her mother.

Juanita and I have never treated her like she is our sister, always like she is our daughter. To this day I can't remember she is my sister. I will say at any given time, "Baby is there anything Auntie can do for you?"

Her reply, "Girl you are not my Aunt you are my sister." It's like she is one of my other sisters daughters.

When I got married Willa was in diapers. Had she been a little older I would have made her my flower girl in my wedding.

Willa went to the same high school as two of my sons, and at the same time. One of my sons was in the tenth grade, one in the eleventh grade, and Willa was in the twelfth grade. All those in high school who did not personally know them thought they were brothers and sister instead of aunt and nephew.

Willa is a loving and caring young lady to all of her family. She has always been there for us at the drop of a dime. We will always be grateful.

Atty Murphy, Lil' Mama, Age 12
My Visit Down South–*1959*

The Third Child of Rosie Walker
Lil' Mama is narrating her own storyline of herself.

I am the third born of Hanspard and Rosie Lee Walker. When we arrived in Los Angeles in 1947, I was still in the oven waiting to be the first kid born in a big city and growing up on 33rd Street in Los Angeles.

As a small child including now, I always was an early riser and to wake up to the smell of my mother cooking bacon and perking coffee for Daddy was the best two smells as a child or adult. I use to be right under my mother when my older sisters went to school. I wanted to learn how to do what she was doing.

Mama had fashion—she would not go downtown shopping without being suited and booted with her gloves on. We always wanted to dress and look poised as we entered a room, just like our mother. Our mother always dressed us well. I use to sneak some of my sisters clothes she purchased from a store that was called The House of Nine, but something was missing and that was accessories. I overdo it with the accessories but that is my signature.

Sometimes I would sit with a smile on my face thinking about when I was a young teenager and when mama had somewhere to go, she would yell to my second oldest sister and tell her to keep me out of her flour and sugar. As soon as my sister would go in the bedroom and shut the door, baking cakes and cookies was on. I never tried to eat my pastries I used my two youngest sisters as my guinea pigs and would sit back laughing while they tasted that horrible mess I had put together.

I can remember my mother's father became ill and Mama was going to her southern home town to be with him and I was chosen to go with her on the train to help with my youngest two sisters. I can recall my Dad on several occasions telling my mom not to take me because I may get her family lynched. At that time I had no idea what my dad was talking about.

We boarded the train at the Union Station, downtown Los Angeles and I as well as many kids were happy and playful but when we got to El Paso, Texas all the blacks had to go to the back of the train and when I asked mama why did we have to go to the back of the train, she just told me to hush up.

I recall Mama briskly grabbing my arm while in the south because I did not call another white female kid ma'am. I was confused and I asked Mama what did I do? Mom said I was supposed to say yes ma'am to the white girl. I told Mama I am not trying to be disrespect to you but I am not going to say yes ma'am to a girl and she is twelve years old like me. I heard Mama say, "Maybe your father was right, I should have left you in California."

Our grandfather's health was declining and Mama did not want to keep me out of school any longer with the school semester just starting. I was told all about the southern rules of what I could do and could not do. Some white girls would stone us and absolutely nothing was done about it. One day a rock or a stone hit me on the side of my left eye and I saw my blood coming out, and they were throwing stones at my cousins and my friends who was my age also.

My cousins and friends they took and ran off and left me. I went over to where the two white girls were and gave them a good old–fashion butt whipping and as I struck them I reminded them that I was from Cali and this mess do not fly by me. I went to school with Whites, Asians, Latinos and I had never experienced prejudice before from kids in school.

As I was running back to my grandfather's farm I said to myself maybe this is why Daddy told Mama not to take me down south. Mama, Aunt Sang and a few more family members hid me and I road with a relative to El Paso, Texas where Daddy met me to take me back to California. Yes I was smuggled back to Cali and it was many years later I realized why none of the black kids who lived in the south did not fight back.

I loved the experience of living on a farm and I think every child should experience it. I was gasping for breath when I first arrived. Our grandfather still had a well, no electricity, wood burning stove, chickens, cows and a stream nearby to fish. Across the road, they called it the woods, was where you would go to hunt for meat.

My sisters said as I grew older how much I am like our mother, and that is a good thing for me to hear. I never started a fight but if you bought it I would accommodate you.

I must say I was a little rascal and it took all of parenting skills to raise me plus a village. One thing about it God and my Mother never gave up on me no matter what adventure I embarked upon.

The Freeway Crawler—1962

In 1962 my husband had just picked up our two babies from Mom's house. They are a year apart. One of the babies was two months old and the other fourteen months old. Seat belts were not invented in the state of California in those days. You either placed your baby into a bassinet on the back seat of the car or place the baby on a blanket.

My husband entered the Harbor Freeway South, but today it is called the 110 Freeway. In 1962, the speed limit posted on the freeways were 75 miles per hour, he was driving about 85 miles per hour.

My husband said he noticed our fourteen month old baby jumping up and down going from one side to the other side in the back seat. He said he thought he was playing and having fun. Husband, our fourteen month old baby could not talk and was probably trying to let you know his little two month old baby brother had fell out of the back car door.

My husband said all of a sudden he heard the right back door clicking back and forth as if it was opened. He said he looked back, and our youngest baby was missing out of the car. He did not have a clue as to where he lost our baby on the freeway. In those days we lived near the Forum in Inglewood, CA.

He was minutes away from Manchester which was the exit off the freeway to get to our house. He exited Manchester and re-entered the freeway headed back to his beginning point of entry. Returning he got into the slowest lane trying to see if he could see anything connected to our baby. Driving for ten minutes he noticed a crowd of people and a white lady had our baby in her arms.

I don't know if my husband's brain freaked out or what, but instead of going to the nearest phone and calling an ambulance or having someone else do it, he bought our baby home. Our house was not more than eight minutes from the freeway.

He knocked on our door and when I opened the door he said, "Sugar Lump look what happened to our baby."

I screamed. I cannot remember if my sister Juanita was over my house or another family member. After all it was fifty-four years ago. Whatever family member was at my house, I told them to call Mama and let her know what happened and I am on my way to the hospital.

I was driving like a bat out of hell. As I rushed into the emergency room I saw Mama pacing the floor back and forth as if she had a wife in the delivery room. I was so nervous because I know how Mama is if she thinks any one tried to harm her children or grandchildren.

They had my baby in the back and the nurse was asking me questions about my baby such as what is he allergic to and other things. Before I could answer all the questions Mama walked over to me and gently moved me to the side and said, "Don't worry Baby, Mama will take care of this." I don't want Mama to take care of nothing. If something happens to my baby, she is going to take care of it alright.

How did I know if she was not going to make my husband vanish into thin air if my baby expired?

My husband was seated and looking in disbelief. Mama said to the nurse, "I want you to help my grandbaby, but do you see that man sitting over there, he is my daughter's husband and my grandbaby's father. Nurse have you ever heard of a father losing his own baby out of a car on the freeway and don't know it? My daughter should have checked that man's family background before she married him—there has got to be some insanity in his family somewhere."

Even if the nurse never heard of a baby flying out of a car on the freeway I was so glad she did not agree with Mama—that would have made it worst.

As young and poor as we were fifty-four years ago, with two babies back to back, where was I going to get some money to pay a private investigator to check his family history to see if there was any insanity in his family?

My baby was kept at the hospital for five hours while they did all kinds of test to see if he had brain damage and everything. They could not find one thing wrong with my baby. The doctor talked to me giving me certain instructions about the care of the baby and what signs to watch for. He let me know if he starts vomiting to bring him back immediately, to make sure there is no internal bleeding

Mama said, "Child, it must be a miracle from God because there is no way a baby is going to fall out of a car door with it going that fast, fly through the air and land like a feather."

My mother never knew how to drive a car but if something happens to one of her children or grandchildren, she always managed to get there before the people with the cars. Very strange!

Mama came home with me and my husband and she decided to stay a few days to keep an eye on her grandbaby—my husband and I were not happy about that.

I was trying to get her to go home but failed. My husband was not about to ask her to go home. Very wise decision, hubby, because if her grandbaby expires she is going to have you on the floor out for the count, just with her bare hands not even a weapon.

Mama got a rocking chair and set it close to my baby's bed and made her some type of cushion from a quilt and some pillows. She looked at my husband with a mean look and said, "You'd better hope this baby live through the night." When she said that I thought silently to myself, if my little baby expires my Mama is going to take my husband off the face of this earth and I am going to have three loses. My husband is going to be taken off the face of the earth, my Mama is going to be in jail, and my little baby is going to be in heaven.

My baby from the time he arrived home from the hospital never did look or act as if he had any injury. Mama nicknamed my baby *The Freeway Crawler*. When he comes over or calls her on the phone she says, "Is that my *Freeway Crawler*?"

Mama Dancing to Joe Tex 'Ain't Gonna Bump No More'—1977

In the 1977, Joe Tex was on Soul Train singing his hit song *I Ain't Gonna Bump No More (With No Big Fat Woman)*. Mama thought the lyrics in the song was funny. Every time she heard him sing it she would laugh.

Mama Rosie was at one of her daughters house parties back in the 1970's and someone put on Joe Tex big hit record *I Ain't Gonna Bump No More (With No Big Fat Woman)*—some little skinny man walked over and asked Mama to dance. They started to do the dance called the 'The Bump, which was the latest dance out.

Mama started dancing and bumped her hip onto his hip. When she did that he went across the room. With her strength I was surprise she did not send him through the stucco wall and out onto the lawn. Because he was so young I bet he thought he could out dance her. Wrong!

He later walked over to the couch where mama was sitting and said "Mrs. Walker I don't want to dance with you anymore." Everybody thought that was so funny they could not stop laughing.

One day if you have time go online to YouTube, type in *I Ain't Going To* Bump No More. Pick the one where Joe Tex is doing a live performance on Soul Train—1977. You will see Don Cornelius step to the microphone and introduce Joe Tex and his latest hit. While Joe is singing his latest hit a large size lady walks up onto the stage and started doing the dance The Bump with him. She bumped her big hips so hard to his little hips she knocked him down to the floor—Joe started rubbing his hips and laughing as he got up. When Mama saw that she laughed so hard. I must admit it was very funny.

Ethel Mae Won On Two Different TV Game Shows Two Years In A Row—1980s

Yes, in the early 1980's I was on two different TV game shows two years in a row and won on both and on the third year was on another but it got cancelled out before aired.

In the early 1980's the Times Newspaper, I can't remember what section, had all these new TV game shows that were looking for contestants. I saw one in the newspaper I wanted to try out for and it was called *The Guinness Game*, NBC. I decided to go down and try out for the show. That was the first time I found out there might be as many as four hundred or more people trying out to be picked as a contestant the same day. They were going to pick three contestants out of the many of hundreds that were there. I was one of the three contestants chosen.

The way *The Guinness Game* worked we three contestants were given $1000 each. The one who had the most cash after the game show was over got to keep their cash and take it home. The other two contestants got a consolation price.

There were three acts that were trying to get into the Guinness Book of Records. This game show did not require any brain work just luck. When each of the three acts came up, one at a time, all you had to do is bid as much money of your $1000 as you wanted that they would either succeed or fail. My opponents were bidding their cash just the opposite of me. If they thought the act was impossible the person was going to do, they would bid about $200, not me. I thought the person doing the first act would succeed and bid high, and won. When the next act came up I let my winnings ride. I did the same type of bidding on all three acts and beat out both my opponents by thousands and thousands of dollars.

I went home with thousands of dollars and they went home with a one year supply of something. I can't remember if their consolation prize was worth $500 or less.

With four boys I much rather have thousands of dollars to take home than a $500 consolation prize.

The VCR player had not come out yet when I won on the first TV game show called *The Guinness Game* on NBC. But when I was on *The Price Is Right* on CBS the VCR had just come out and I got to record myself on *The Price Is Right*.

I also learned you could not be on more than three different TV game shows in ten years. Well excuse me I did not know there was a quota. I also learned if you won and your show was cancelled before being aired, you would not get your winnings.

My third show I got picked for on the third year,

What Have You Got To Lose?

We three contestants were playing against an orangutan. We were all seated in at our own classroom desk. A deck of cards was placed on each of our desk face down. On each card was a prize, money, or trip. On the opposite side facing us was an Orangutan in a real King's chair with a King's crown on his head and a cape around his shoulder.

The host would ask a trivia question to each of us one by one. If you got the question right, you would turn the card over and whatever was on the face of card you would win. If you answered the question wrong the orangutan would reach over and take the card from you and place it on his desk. I had the game beat and I did not care if I got the last question right or wrong.

The question was, "What state is Martha's Vineyard?" My brain went blank, I knew it was in an eastern state but could not remember which state. The show was cancelled and never aired.

Don't Walk Up On Mama from the Back—1985

One day Mama was visiting me at my house. In my den she was sitting on one couch and my sister Juanita and I was sitting on the other couch. We noticed her new purse. It looked like it was beat up, scratched, and the pretty gold handle was bent. Juanita had bought her this very expensive pretty purse. We asked her what happened to her purse. She said she was getting ready to go into the store K-Mart to shop on Imperial and Western, in Los Angeles.

Getting closer to the store she saw a man rushing up behind her real fast like he was going to rob her. She said she slowed down on purpose because the only way you are going to get an enemy you have got to let them close to you. How many women do you know who can see they are getting ready to be robbed from the back and slow down on purpose?

She let him get close enough upon her back to reach back and grab him, which she did. She snatched him over her right shoulder and threw him to the ground, jumped on top of him with her knee and leg across his throat pressing as hard as she could and started beating him and hitting him with her purse.

A service station was located very close to K-Marts on the same corner. One of the service station employees yelled at Mom, "I'm coming to help you lady."

Mama said she yelled back, "You ain't got to help me I got this sucker.

The police arrested the man. Not too many weeks later a court date was set for the guy to appear. He was bought out from the back of the court to set in those seats near the judge's bench. I bet the judge and his court room employee's was probably wondering how did this little exactly five feet woman take a big tall man down and out like she did. But they don't know she was born with the strength of ten, otherwise the question would not have entered their minds.

Our mother was funnier than Moms Mabley and any other funny paid professional comedian. "Who is Moms Mabley?" Her name is Jackie 'Moms' Mabley. She was a Comic/Actress born March 19, 1884 and expired May 23, 1975.

In 1939, Mabley made history by becoming the first comedian to play the famed Apollo Theater in Harlem before large crowds.

Ethel Mae's Car Accident—1989

Yes I believe in Angels.

When the 1987 Nissan Maxima came out I thought the car was so pretty with the sunroof that opened at the top. I found out the sticker price for the car was $25,000. I did my homework to see I could do a little negotiation with the salesman to knock the price down a lot lower.

The dealer takes me out onto the lot and let me get behind the stern wheel to test drive. The car drove like a 747 as if you could not feel the wheels touching the road. After I test drove the car I knew I was not leaving off the lot without it. The salesman and I finally reach a negotiable price, far less than the sticker price, and I drove off the lot with my car.

I had the car for not more than two years when I had a strange dream. In my dream underneath the accelerator appeared a long huge silver-spring. The large silver-spring appeared to be the size of my entire arm from the top of my arm to my fingertips. In my dream the stern wheel was vibrating side to side like a wild horse, and I said over and over: "Pain, pain, pain." I woke up in a sweat, I felt something was not right about the car but I did not know what.

I decided to take the car into the Nissan Dealer by my job. I told them a lie because I did not want to tell them about the dream. Did you want them to think I needed to be committed to the 'Funny Farm; my definition for a mental institution.

I said to the Nissan Repairman: "When I drive the car real fast the gas pedal sticks and the stern wheel vibrates in my hands like a wild horse. Maybe you should keep the car a few days to see what the problem is." In those days if you bought a new car from this dealer and they had to keep the car for days, they got you a free rental car to keep until the repairs were done. They checked the car out thoroughly and could not find one thing wrong.

I was still was having bad dreams about the car. I decided not to take the car to the Nissan Dealer by my job again. This time I would take the car to Gardena Nissan in Gardena, California which was close to my house. I told the Nissan repairman the same lie I told the other Nissan repairman by my job. They checked the car out thoroughly again and could not find one single thing wrong with it.

The bad dreams about the car continued. I go back to the Gardena Nissan by my house and asked the salesman if he could find me an identical car like mine if not in this color any color. The 1987 Nissan Maxima was so hot and in demand the salesman could not find another one like mine in my state or any state.

I said I would trade this car in and get the new 1989 Nissan Maxima that just came out. The car salesman takes me out onto the lot to look at the new 1989 Nissan Maxima. I could not believe my eyes the body of the car had totally changed. The new 1989 Maxima body could not touch the beauty of my 1987 body on the best of day. The salesman told me the body like my car was only made in 1987 and 1988. I said forget it, it was just a stupid dream. And that is why I did not buy the new 1989 Nissan Maxima.

It was my son and nephew's nineteenth birthday. I decided to take them to Las Vegas for their birthday. In my car also were two of my sisters, Juanita and Lil' Mama.

Like most people visiting Las Vegas, you gamble and get little or no sleep. On our way back home to Los Angeles, I hit the 15 Freeway and did the one thing our father told us to never do if we are tired and that was—do not set the cruise control because it makes you too relaxed and your thinking impaired. Just as soon as I hit the 15 Freeway, I set the car in cruise control at a speed of eighty-five miles per hour. I do not know at what point I went sound asleep but I felt like I was at home comfortable in my own bed. The police report I read later said we ended up in Bake, California.

Everybody in the car was sound asleep including me, the driver. Juanita's voice is what woke me up with a loud scream, "Ethel!"

She was in the back right seat asleep and she said what woke her up she thought my tires had blown out. When I woke up the car had gone off the road to the left going down a small hill, the stern wheel was vibrating out of control jumping up and down and side to side. It was as if a second voice was talking to me telling me what to do. I tapped the breaks to release the cruise control, grab hold to the stern wheel and held it as tight as I could, which was hard to with it bouncing all over my hand. The car did a perfect U-turn from traveling down the mountain where it started going back up the mountain with all four tires gripping the ground and staying on the ground.

Thank God when the car shot back up onto the asphalt highway there were no other cars. Had there been cars on the highway when I got there, at the speed I was traveling, eight-five miles an hour, there would have been so many fatalities.

The car started traveling to the right straight across the highway. I could see the first flip over into the air and saw the sky out of my window. After that I don't remember anything.

When I woke up it was really quiet in the car and I thought everybody was dead. I felt like I was in a fetus position up in the air with a belt around my waist holding me intact. I was wiggling my legs and arms back and forth and they felt fine with no pain; I was trying to lift my head up to straighten it out, but something was preventing me from lifting my head so that I could sit up in the car straight. All of a sudden I can see a hand coming across my chest. It was my son's voice and he said, "Mama I am getting the key out of the ignition to stop the motor

I passed out again. A strange voice woke me up.

I could hear a strange person's voice outside say, "Lady, we can't get to you and you have got to release your seat belt." I was so out of it I did not know what a seat belt was. It was as if the strange voice knew and then the strange voice said, "Lady feel on your right side going down the seat belt for a button and push the button." I did what the strange voice said and pushed the button. After that I felt like I dropped to the car floor. The strange voice always called me "Lady." And no matter what command the strange voice gave me I always obeyed.

The next thing I can remember is seeing a white arm with fingers stretched out as if reaching for me. The strange voice said, "Lady, grab my hand, which I can clearly remember gripping the person's hand and being dragged but I did not know where. I later found out it was my back car window my only exit out. Because of the way the car first hit the ground and landed down in the ravine tumbling over and over for a hundred yards, it bent my driver's left door frame which prevented me from opening and stepping out like everybody else. It also bent the frame of the seat I was sitting in preventing me from exiting from my front right door.

Once the car settled down everybody in the car was able to unbuckle their seat belt, open their doors and step out; that was not me and Juanita's case. Juanita did not have her seat belt on while we were driving. My sister Lil' Mama said she found

Juanita thrown out the back window and was lying on top of the back hood unconscious. Lil' Mama got Juanita down and laid her on the grown.

When I woke up again I felt like I was lying down on top of a straight wooden board. Something was holding my head down where I could not turn it one way or the other. I felt my forehead and it felt like a piece of tape was over my forehead holding my head to the wood I was lying on.

But I could see out of the right corner of my eyes another wooden board with Juanita on top of it. Two men were standing over her in the same color clothing as the two men standing over me. I could clearly hear one of them say: "I can't get her vital signs we are losing her. I said to the two men standing over me: "I am fine go over and help them with my sister, she is so quiet."

I passed out again, but something woke me up. I felt like I was in a big truck going over a rough highway. When I woke up someone was over me with their fingers running back and forth over my forehead. The voice of this person said, "No, no don't go to sleep."

I said, "Leave me alone I have got to get some rest I am so tire."

The voice and finger thing on top of my forehead repeated itself, "No, no don't go to sleep." At this point I didn't know me and Juanita were in a helicopter being air lifted to the Las Vegas hospital in

Las Vegas.

When I awakened again I could see lots of bright lights above me and lots of people all around me in white clothing. My subconscious mind made me ask them where was my sister Juanita. None replied. I asked the question, "Is she dead?" No reply. I said, "Go and get my sister Lil' Mama." She came over to my bedside looking down at me and I asked her where was Juanita. She said they were getting ready to take her into surgery to locate the bleeding.

I was in the hospital not more than twenty-four hours and Juanita stayed five days. My husband, Daddy, and Mama picked me up and something made me want them to drive over to the tow yard to see my car.

Once I walked over to my car I could see why I could not exit out of my left door or the front right door. The frame to my front left door frame was too bent and the car seat I was sitting in the frame was also bent badly. But my sister Lil' Mama was sitting up front to my right was able to unbuckle her seat belt and step out. When I walked to the back of my wrecked car, the back car window looked as if it popped out when it hit the ground down in the ravine. There was no glass showing as if entire window popped out leaving no glass. That is probably why Juanita and I had no cuts or scratches on us anywhere.

When we all got better my sister Lil' Mama told

us what happened. She said when she stepped out of the car it was so much dust kicking up from our car tumbling she could hardly see anything. All of a sudden she could clearly see a white man and a white lady walking through the dust approaching our car. She said they were the first ones to get there to help us before help arrived.

Lil' Mama could see some men in black or very dark navy-blue shirts and pants trying to work their way down the mountain and ravine trying to get to us. She said they were men from the ambulance.

Lil' Mama said the ambulance driver told her they were coming from a previous accident and knew nothing about our accident and something told him to stop in that spot and look down the ravine. She said as they were approaching the white man and the white lady disappeared. No one knew how they arrived nor did anyone see them leave.

There was only two ways out, either the helicopter would have had to land down in the ravine and air lift them out like they did me and Juanita or they would have needed some ropes and equipment to get up and down the mountain of the ravine. There was no other way out.

To this day Juanita and I do not remember anything about a white man or a white lady.

Tenors, Cook, Dixon, & Young, with Rosie Walker—2003

Rosie Lee Walker with her Great-Great nephew, Tenor Rodrick Dixon (far left)

The year was 2003 when The Tenors were performing at the Cerritos Center, Cerritos, California which was no more than thirty-five minutes from my house. One day Mom opened her mail and in the envelope were four complimentary tickets from her great-nephew Robert Black. She called me over to the dining room table and said, "Ethel Mae, look what I got in the mail from my great-nephew Robert." Her facial expression became so happy. The four tickets were for Mom and three of her daughters. Also in the envelope were backstage passes for all of us to pin on our clothes. The seats were very good seats, we were seated tenth row center. We have never liked sitting the first few rows in the center, too close to the stage.

Not only was Mom excited to meet The Tenors for the first time—she became more excited when she saw her two nephews, Robert Black and Tenor Rodrick. As excited and happy as she was acting you would have thought she had just won a two million dollar lottery ticket. Mom's great-nephew, Tenor Rodrick Dixon, have a beautiful voice also the other two men who sings in the group with him, Victor Trent and Thomas Young. Their voices blended well together.

They sang lots of old songs, but one song they asked the audience to sing along with them was *Minnie The Moocher* recorded by Cab Calloway in 1931.

Mama stood up in front of her seat and sang along with them and started doing some of those 1930's and 1940's dance moves, before I was born. She was moving from side to side and making her hand move to the rhythm. She was eighty-three years old in 2003. Do you know she knew every word to Cab Calloway's 1931 song about *Minnie The Moocher*. The only lyrics I knew to the song are Hi-De-Hi-De-Ho and not another word.

The Dog And Cow Story—2004

Our World War II father, Hanspard Walker, had a stroke in 2001 and had become very ill. Because of Daddy's illness the family had to take him to the doctor far too often, and he had some stays in the hospital. After his stroke his Alzheimer began. Eventually his Alzheimer got worst, but he recognized his immediate family and could go back in time and remember things you have forgotten, but his memory was not good on present things. Daddy had gotten so bad until he had to be placed in a nursing home for the kind of care he needed.

One day I was visiting him at the nursing home and sitting by his bedside in a chair. All of a sudden I noticed he started laughing to himself. I said, "Daddy what are you laughing about?"—"Ethel Mae, about you the dog and the cow."—"And what about me the dog and the cow?" He started to tell me a story I had not heard before. Listening to the story I could not have been too much older than two years old because I was old enough to talk, but not old enough to put all the words in the right place. It all happened between 1945 and 1946, before we moved to Los Angeles. At that time we lived in the woods of Louisiana.

Daddy said one day he picked me up and took me and my little puppy out to the cow pasture with him. When my little puppy saw the baby calf he started running back and forth barking and playing with the calf. He said the cow thought my little puppy was harming his baby. The cow came over, stepped on top of my little puppy and killed him. Daddy said I reversed the words and said "the dog killed the cow." I looked over to Daddy and said, "The stupid cow killed my puppy." "Yes."—"Daddy you know how I have this mental thing every time I see a little dead dog on the street or highway since I was a very little child. You know that might be the reason." He came back, "could be." Do you know after Daddy told me the story about the dog and the cow, I got better. I wished he had told me the story before 2004.

All my life, up until Daddy told me the story, if I saw a dead dog on the ground, my entire body acts as if I had just run over my own child. I have to fight back the tears and get very sad. Often times I do not know the owner or the dog.

In 2002 Mama and I was in my car on the way to some family event and on the highway was a dead dog lying on the side of the road and I saw it. The first words out of Mama's mouth, "Gal, I see you acting funny because you see the dead dog on the side of the road. You'd better pull yourself together and don't try to kill me in this car. And don't start crying, you did not kill the dog and you don't know the dog."

Daddy's Funeral—2004

It was supposed to be a Daddy's day, how did me and my sisters know Mama was going to steal the show?

Have you ever been to an over-the-top funeral? We have—our father's funeral in 2004. Our mother Rosie was the one who made Daddy's funeral a lot more over-the-top than the funeral scene in the 2001 movie 'Kingdom Come where in the church scene Jada Pickett played the role of the crazy daughter-in-law. The movie starred Whoopi Goldberg.

We all drove to Daddy and his second wife's house in Los Angeles to wait for the funeral cars to pick us up. While Mama and all her daughters were sitting around their dining room table someone passed a few obituaries to us. Mama and all of us read the obituary and saw there was no mentioning of Mama's name on the obituary and the way the obituary was printed up you would have thought Daddy' s daughters was his second wife's children.

The funeral cars pulled up in front of Daddy's house and we all got into the cars headed for the church. Seated on one side of the church was the family and on the other side the visitors. My sisters and I did not sit in the first row center with Daddy's present wife we sit in the third row with Mama.

None of Daddy and his wife's church members

ever saw Mama before. I bet Daddy and his present wife's minister and church members were all trying to figure out why are all of Brother Walker's daughters sitting in a row so far back away beside this strange woman instead of sitting in the front row with Daddy's present wife, who they thought was our real mother. They probably thought we were horrible daughters because we never go by to check on our mother. Wrong! My sisters and I have treated our Mom like she was Queen Elizabeth all of our lives. Our Mama Rosie is more spoiled than a new born baby. She was a surprised born child and her parents, siblings and our father spoiled her rotten. I do not know if Mama heard the word no in her life. I am surprised she turned out to be so sweet and given with all that spoiled stuff for her entire life.

The Minister steps to the microphone and make the announcement, "Everybody who comes up to speak on Brother Walker are given two minutes to speak."

Mama turns her head and looks at me and said, "Ethel Mae, I am going to get up and give a big talk on Hamp—dad's nickname. I have got to let the church know when y'all were little children he came in jealous and threw that big pot of stew on the floor I cooked for my children and I took and chunked him out the window. I want God and Hamp to forgive me." The word chunked in the South means threw.

As her oldest daughter I could not let her get up to the microphone and tell the Daddy and his wife's church members how she chunked him out the window. Forgive me God but I am getting ready to lie for the first time in church.

"Mama, God and Daddy forgave you a long time ago."

She said, “You reckon?”

And I said, "Yes.”

She said, “Ok Baby."

How would I know I was only five years old, Juanita was three years, and the other three sisters were not born? How would any of us know? And who would have thought she was carrying that guilt around in her brain all these years in the first place.

It was time for all of us to walk around to view Daddy's body in the casket. After viewing my sisters and I returned to our seats, but Mama was missing, she was supposed to be in front of me on the return. We looked up and could not believe our eyes. Mama was in front of Daddy's casket rubbing his face all romantic with his wife sitting in front of the casket. Mama dropped to the floor, screaming and carrying on real loud. Two of Daddy and his wife's ushers walked over to Mom and grabbed her from each side, lifted her up from on the floor because she did not want to let go of Daddy's casket. All the way down the aisle with the two ushers on both sides of her trying to keep her from going limp.

Her voice was sounding as loud as Patti Labelle where you could hear her inside the church to the next country. "Hamp, Hamp what am I going to do without you, I ain't never going to see you again." She was taking it harder than every family member in the church.

At this point I was sure all of Daddy and his wife's church members were thinking this must be Daddy's girlfriend. The Pastor gets up from his seat and steps to the microphone and says it twice, "Please respect the family, please respect the family." Everybody was respecting the family except the strange woman they did not know who was carrying on like it was a movie scene being filmed—we call her Mama.

If I knew Mama was going to carry on at Daddy's funeral like that I would have had them give me a microphone and put me on the roof to hear the funeral service.

We get to the burial site at the cemetery and the immediate family was seated in chairs in front of Daddy's casket. The Minister started walking to each family member seated shaking their hands and giving his condolence. He gets to Mama, who is seated next to me, shakes her hand and gives his condolence. When he gets to me he added a few more words that I have never heard for a condolence. He dropped his head down close to my head and left ear, shaking my hand and giving me my condolence, but all the time his head was turned to Mama. Out of his mouth came these words, "Ethel, who is this lady sitting next to your?"

I tried to say it as loud as I could, "our mother." Don't think our mother is some kind of little hooker who sleeps around with men.

Later that night I get a call from my baby sister Willa and she said, "Girl, as loud as you said 'our mother'—everybody heard you." And then she said, "Well, I guess everyone knows who our real mother is now."

I replied, "You got them apples right."

The next couple of days I started to get all these calls from our relatives in Louisiana who had gotten back how Mama carried on at Daddy's funeral.

"Ethel Mae, we heard about Aunt Rosie, is it true she did all of that at Uncle Hamp's funeral?"

"Oh yes she stole the show.

"Aunt Rosie is so funny."

What Is A Sheet Shaker—2006

I took Mom to see one of her doctors, and he asked her, "Rosie, how are you doing?"

"Oh doctor I'm batting a million, but I am looking for me a *Sheet Shaker*."

"What is a *Sheet Shaker*?"

"Child, you don't know what a *Sheet Shaker* is?"

"No."

"That is a man," like everybody is supposed to know what a *Sheet Shaker* is.

The doctor takes his scratch pad out of his pocket and writes on it *Sheet Shaker* is a man. "Mrs. Walker, when I go home and walk into my house, I am going to say to my wife, 'Honey your *Sheet Shaker* is here.' Mrs. Walker, I know she is going to ask me what is a *Sheet Shaker.*"

All of Mom's doctors loved her and her story telling.

Often times, when the doctor is done with her and tells her to dress, if he is not too busy with another patient he will rush back into her room before she leaves to hear one more of Mom's back-in-the-day stories. She would say, "Child you better get back with those other patients."

She never could say the word "*prosecute*," instead she always said the word "*prostitute.*" If she was watching the news on TV and they catch the person who kidnapped or harmed a child, Mama would say, "I hope they *prostitute* that sucker, killing that little baby like that."

Surprise Visitors At My House But I Am Not Home—2008

My sister Juanita and I decided to go shopping at Walmart. We were not gone longer than two hours. We asked Mom if she wanted to go. She said "no." We left her at my house.

When we returned to my house as I got closer to the house I saw an ambulance, fire wagon, and police car parked in front of my house. Juanita and I knew there must be something seriously wrong with Mama. We jumped out of my car and did a hundred yard dash into my house—like we can do a hundred yard dash in our sixties like we did when we were fifteen. Not! We were all out of breath from running as fast as we could.

I opened my front door and seated at the head of my dining room table was Mom surrounded by two ambulance drivers, two paramedics, and two police officers. Mom was talking to them but I could not hear what she was saying and all of them were laughing out of control.

Juanita was so out of breath from the run she went over to my couch and stretched out trying to get her breath. She looked like she was about to have an asthma attack.

I asked them why they were here. They said Mama called them and why. I asked them what was the matter with my Mama—they said nothing. I came back with, "Then why are you here?"

Juanita's breathing had gotten so rapid that one of the paramedics asked her is there anything he could do for her. She told him no. I jumped in and these were the exact words out of my mouth, "We are not the patient, the one you are having the party with at my table is the patient."

Our Mom has been a diabetic since the age of seventy-three. She never tested her sugar, I always do. I do not know if she was having a senior moment or not. On the Glucose Monitoring Machine's box is a code and the code number on the box was 708. With the machine if you want to know if the code is correct, you take out a test trip, without blood on it, and stick it into the machine and the code number 708 will show up on the monitory which is the same number on the box.

I had just tested Mom's sugar in the morning, like I always did. Her glucose levels are never over 130 before eating. What Mama did, she took out the test strips and did not put any blood on it, inserted the test strip into the machine and when the code number 708 came up on the monitor she thought her sugar level was too high. She dropped the machine and dialed 911.

As they exited the door one or two of them said, "We hate to go because we can listen to your mother talk all day, she is so funny."

"Yes I know, she was born very unique."

When they walked out the door I looked at her with a facial expression meaning—oh no, you didn't. You know the woman can read folks minds because after looking at my face she came back with "better safe than sorry."

Another Blessing By The Williams Brother—2007

When the CD, *Crazy Like Love* came out in 2007 by The Williams Brother, Mama had me buy it. She loved the gospel music by The Williams Brothers. Ethel Mae put my boys CD on with *Another Blessing* and play it for me."

The music was at an upbeat tempo and if you remove the religious words, you could boogie. Mama must have removed the religious words and was listening to the upbeat tempo. At first I thought she had gotten the Holy Ghost and was getting ready to do that type of dance. I was wrong. All of a sudden she grabbed one of my hands and started making some moves, before I was born. I think she was having one of those 1930—1940 flashbacks. The moves she was making were one of the jitter bug type of dances back in the Cab Calloway and Louis Armstrong days.

"Mama, check yourself this is not that kind of music."

"Oh, Baby you are right. Who knows, she might have had another senior moment and thought it was 1940 in Louisiana at one of those juke joints in the woods."

Kissing Cousins and Betsy Bugs

What is a Betsy Bug? Passalidae is a family of beetles known as "bessbugs","bess beetles", "betsy beetles" or "horned passalus beetles."

Mama said if you marry your own cousin and have babies every one of them might turn out as crazy as a Betsy bug. It sounded as if Mama was saying a lady's name of Betsy or Bessie. Down South where my family lived, when visiting—I have heard that a lot growing up. At first I thought it was one of the sayings carried down from slavery days or they got it from a book. When I started to school and was old enough to read I thought I would look in an encyclopedia or dictionary see if there was a such a bug, I could not find it in the books in the early 1950's.

In 2014, I decided to go online to see if there was a Betsy bug. Yes there is such a bug. Stupid me, I thought it was another one of those old southern saying that were not in any books.

Making Fun of Anything While Pregnant Is Not A Good Thing

Mama said you should never make fun of anyone when you are in your first stage of pregnancy. She said if you do your baby might come here looking like whatever living thing you were looking at and making fun of.

She said there was a lady in her town that looked just like a mule. Come to find out when her mother was pregnant a mule scared her and the mother jumped. Mama thinks that is why the lady looked like a mule her entire life. Mama said some children will outgrow it quickly but some will look like that forever

Mom said when she was in her beginning stage of pregnancy with her last daughter—a movie was released in 1958 called The Fly, starring Vincent Price. In the movie there was a scientist doing experimental stuff in his glass chamber. One day he opened the door to his glass chamber and closed it for whatever experiment he was trying. He did not know a fly had gotten into the chamber with him. Some kind of scientific way the fly ended up having a human head but still looked like a little fly.

There was a scene where it showed the little fly on a leaf on a bush in the yard, and you could see the human head attached to the fly. In the scene you could see the little fly's mouth was open and coming out of his mouth you could hear the fly say over and over "help me somebody, help me somebody." Mama said that one scene scared her and made her jump.

When my baby sister Willa was born she had a little funny looking tongue like the fly in the movie. Mama had to have her tongue clipped, after that she had a pretty tongue. Mama thought that was the reason Willa was born with her tongue like that.

Thank *God* Willa is a pretty lady and never looked like a fly. Listening to Mama about stuff like that, she could have come here looking like a fly and maybe forever.

Grandma Held Off A Robber—2009

In 2009, we were watching the TV news about an eighty-nine year old grandmother who held off a robber who broke into her house. On the news you could see the news reporter put the microphone to her mouth while she told what happened.

Grandma said she could hear someone breaking into her front door. She reached underneath her bed and pulled out her .22 gun, laid down on the floor close to the front door where he could not see her.

When he got in the door, she said she cocked her trigger and made him lay face down in front of her couch, all the time with the gun pointed at his head. She backed around to the other side of the couch, never taking the gun off him. When she got behind the couch she said she stretched her hand over the couch, with her gun in it, and kept it pointed down at his head while he was on the floor. I cannot remember if she said she called the police or made him call.

She said it looked like the police took forever to come. From keeping her arm stretched out over the couch with the gun, the arthritis in her hand and arm starting hurting real bad.

Just as soon as I saw the news on TV about the Grandma and the robber breaking into her house, I immediately thought of my eighty-eight year old Mama Rosie.

The only similarity the TV Grandma had to my Mama Rosie Lee were, yes Mama would have been in her house waiting for the police to come and that is the only thing she would have done like the TV Grandma.

There was no way anyone was going to make my Mama's arthritis flare up and hurt in any part of her body. Our mother would have been stretched out on her couch comfortable, watching either her judges or her stories. Mama was not going to kill him but when she got through with him he would have wished he was dead. And whatever she did it was going to be legal and not against the law.

The Last Days Of Rosie Lee Walker—2015

In 2001, Mom moved in with me, she was happy to stay with her oldest daughter Ethel Mae. In 2002, when she was eighty-two years old she was diagnosed with left breast cancer.

Mom did not have her breast removed but instead she had a lumpectomy, was given radiation, and prescribed an oral chemotherapy tablet by the name of Arimidex (Anastrozole) at 1 mg oral a day. The usual protocol for the patient was to be kept on this oral tablet for five years, or is it six years, and if the cancer does not come back the doctor will discontinue the drug.

For thirteen years Mom had no reoccurrence of her cancer. In 2015, when she was ninety-four years old, her cancer returned like a wild tornado hitting with a devastating force.

On February 2015, I was admitted into the hospital a few days with pneumonia. My sister Juanita kept Mom for a few weeks while I recovered. One day, while I was recovering at home, I get a call from Juanita. She said Mama woke up in the morning with terrible pain all over her body. She said she called the ambulance to take her to the hospital. She was admitted and they ran all kinds of tests. The results of the test came back with cancer of the bones, one of the worst. They gave her six months to live. The hospital discharged her the next day and we brought her home where I could care for her.

I had Hospice come out to my house to help me care for Mom. She expired two months after she was diagnosed with bone cancer, February 13, 2015.

Our mother, like most Southerners in our town, have the belief when it is time for you to go Home to Glory, some of your loved ones will appear in front of you to help you go Home to Glory. One night I was sound asleep and Mom's voice woke me up from her bedroom which is very close to mine. To me it sounded as if she was having a nightmare. The closer I got to her bedroom I could hear these words out of her mouth, "Mama and Virginia are you sending the car for me?" She was talking to her mother and her daughter. I thought to myself, she is having a nightmare. Mom's mother Virginia Edwards expired in 1933 when Mom was thirteen years old. Mom's daughter Virginia Marie Walker Jones expired in 1982 at the age of twenty-nine years old. In other words, there are two Virginia's.

When I got to Mom's bedroom I gently touched her shoulder to wake her up. "Mama, who are you talking to?"

"Nobody."

When I heard her call out to Grandma Virginia and my sister Virginia I knew that was a very bad sign and your days left on this earth are few.

Because our Mother Rosie was born with a *Veil Over Her Head* and could foresee things and be dead on target all of her life, I believe she knew the days she had left on this earth were few. You believe what you want and family will believe what we want. Mom has always called it like it is.

One day my baby sister Willa drove down to spend a few weekend days with me to help with Mom so I could get some rest. She slept in Mom's bed next to her and while Mom was sound asleep she heard the same thing I did come out of Mom's mouth. "Mama and Virginia, are you sending the car for me?"

There was another weekend day my baby sister Willa drove to my house to give me a little help with mom so I could get some rest. Early in the morning Willa comes to my room and she said, "Ethel Mae, below Mama's knuckles on her hands all of her fingers has turned white and is as cold as ice and sweat is pouring off her body." I immediately got out of bed and went to her room to examine her, sure enough Willa called it. Below her knuckles on each hand had turned white and was as cold as ice.

I did not want to tell my baby sister Willa, but that was a very bad sign her organs were shutting down.

I called the ambulance and we follow behind in Willa's car on the way to Mission Hospital, not more than eight minutes from my house. Mom was admitted on April 12, 2015, she expired on April 13, 2015 at 2,00 a.m.

You have no idea how glad I was my mother was with me except for one day. She never spent a day in a nursing home. Thank you Lord.

Rosie Lee Edwards-Walker Funeral April 25, 2015

Sunrise, September 3, 1920
Sunset, April 13, 2015

Mama's funeral was held on Saturday, April 25, 2015, at Inglewood Park Cemetery, Inglewood, California in the Galleria Chapel.

The officiating Pastor was Pastor Tommy Stewart at Reach Community Church, Lake Forest, California. Pastor Tommy Stewart is our Mama Rosie Walker and her daughters Ethel Mae and Juanita pastor.

The chapel seats 300 people, if I had to guess there had to been 400 hundred people or more because so many were standing on the walls and outside who could not get in. Mama always said she could draw a crowd from the early age of five.

Pastor Tommy's eulogy and sermon on our Mother Rosie was off the chain. The way he delivered his sermon was spiritual but funny. When he spoke and gave his sermon on Mama he read her to a T. She was a very funny lady who could make you fall out on the floor laughing. The way Pastor Tommy delivered the sermon you would have thought we were in Las Vegas at a famous comedian's show.

Mama's funeral was the first I have ever attended or heard of where everybody in the audience laughed out of control. Any story he told on her had you falling out of your seat laughing.

We cannot remember the entire sermon Pastor Tommy gave, but we still remember when he said, "Back-in-the-day Mother Walker use to walk around packing, in the name of *Jesus*." Oh yes, Pastor did add at the end "in the name of *Jesus*." The way he said it people laughed harder.

Pastor Tommy said he looked in the Old Testament and the New Testament and even looked somewhere that was not his religious denomination and he could not find anything where it says it is okay to go around packing a gun in your purse.

I do not know how she got a license to carry a gun in her purse legally. She was born with something that makes people say yes to anything she wants. Oh yes, the lady was born very unique, definitely Guinness book of records material. I shall assure you some of the things she has done in her life have never been done by any human on this earth in history. Her persuasion for getting anything she wants is probably the best I have seen.

One Sunday, Pastor Tommy and his wife Portia

stood at the front door to greet the members as they exited the front door when church was over. Mama walked over to the Pastor's wife and said it real loud, "You'd better watch your man, I'm here."

Pastor and his wife laugh so hard when she said it. Giving his sermon about Mama Pastor Tommy said, "My wife do not mind me kissing and hugging Mother Walker."

One day in 2014 Mama was looking at the news on TV. The news reporter said during church service on Sunday some men in masks broke into the Baptist Church in Los Angeles with guns and masks and robbed some of the church members.

Mama said, "Ethel Mae, if we are at our church, let 'em come up in here on us—the Lord said to be ready. I would have had them running like a turkey through the corn with his long draws on."

Pearls of Wisdom To The Edwards and Walker Family

Because we have forgotten our Ancestors our children no longer gives us honor.

Because we have lost the path our Ancestors, our children cannot find their way.

Because we have banished the **God** of our Ancestors our children cannot pray.

Because we have abandoned our wisdom of mothering and fathering, our befuddled children give birth to children they never wanted or understood.

Because we have forgotten how to love, the adversary is within our gates, and holds us up to the mirror of the world, shouting no regards for love.

In honor of those who toiled and implored **God** we golden tongues and in gratitude. To the same **God** who brought us out of hopeless desolation, we have this pledge.

We the family of today salute our forefathers for giving us a strong foundation.

We thank you for never giving up when there was so much despair and little hope.

We thank you for a long history of strong morals and religious values.

We thank you for passing on the professional and athletic skills that you never had a chance to show.

We thank you most of all for teaching us to be **God** fearing and giving us the ability to show compassion, understanding and love one another.